Starving Writers
Literary Journal

Volume 1

"The Writer's Journey"

January 2019

Starving Writers Literary Journal- Volume 1

January 2019

A Truesource Publishing Book

Truesource Publishing : Dallas Texas

www.truesourcepublishing.com

ISBN : 978-1-932996-67-8

Printed in the United States of America
Published in Dallas, Texas

Editors
Marcus Blake
Jenn Chastka
Camila Gonzalez
Andrew Fallman

For More information on Starving Writers…

www.starvingwriters.net
www.facebook.com/starvingwritersjournal
www.twitter.com/starvingwritersjournal

"There is nothing to writing. All you do is sit down at a typewriter and bleed."

~ Ernest Hemingway

Table of Contents

From the Editor

The Birth of Starving Writers...

It's true, just like the quote on the front of the journal, writing is a journey. And the same definitely goes for a literary journal. For us, at Starving Writers, we are excited for the journey and invite you to come along. We believe that words and ideas can change the world... it's like our unofficial motto, but is seems as if the idea is rooted in our DNA when it comes to our passion for literature. That, I think, is the genesis for the journal. However, it's more than that. Part of the philosophy of Starving Writers is that this is a place for writers to come together and share ideas without the fear of being censored. It's a place for writers to get their start. Their words are more than just published; they are put out into the world, waiting to be discovered.   Every writer has to start somewhere and learn their craft in order to be good at it. And in a world filled with more rejection than acceptance, Starving Writers is a good place start.

We didn't start this to be rich. In fact money doesn't really matter as long as this journal is still around. The words, they are the most important than everything else. They will live on far longer than any of us. I'd like to think this journal is a record…a record of all that can be possible in literature. A journal filled with voices that will always be heard and never quieted. For if words and ideas can truly change the world, then they must be allowed to thrive. And, that is our true mission at Starving Writers. If you love literature, come with on this journey, and discover new and amazing authors. For writers, share the road with us in our literary journey. Dare to go where you have never been. With your words, you are the misfits that help keep the motor of the world running.

~ Marcus Blake

"So here's my idea: have my novel be about a freelance writer
who spends too much time on social media and
not enough time writing. That way I'm doing
RESEARCH and ta-daaah...No more guilt!"

Check out more cartoons like this….
www.inkygirl.com

INKYGIRL.COM: Dailiy Diversions For Writers
Copyright©2007 Debbie Ridpath Ohi

Check out more cartoons like this….
www.inkygirl.com

SHORT STORIES

CHIMERA

By

Jason DeGray

Eurich ripped open the package with unbridled excitement. It had finally come! He got the DNA Holovid for his birthday and had been saving his allowance to buy a slide for it. The outer packaging torn away, he started working on the box. His mind raced with the possibilities: lion, alligator, wolf, eagle, elephant. There were so many great choices he didn't know which he wanted more. He'd spent days memorizing the Ancient Latin names of his favorites, so he'd know which one he got right out of the box. Finally the moment came when he ripped open the box and pulled out the smooth glass slide. His eyes, alight with excitement moments before, extinguished in pools of disappointment.

"Koo…koo…lus…Can…orus? What in all the Graces is a *Cuculus canorus*?"

"No swearing young man," said his father without looking away from his eye screen, his deft fingers punching buttons in thin air never missing a beat. "And it's a cuckoo bird."

"A cuckoo bird? What a bunch of dip."

"I said no swearing! Why don't you go try it out? It may be more blazin than you think."

"Whatever," Eurich clomped to his room and slammed the door behind him. He reverently pulled the DNA Holovid off his shelf and set it on the floor. He sat next to it and clicked it on. A holographic image of Curio, the built in helpware, sprang up from the pedestal.

"Hello and thank you for your interest in DNA Holovid! DNA Holovid, bringing the lost past to life! Do you have a slide?"

"Yes."

"Blazin! Please insert the slide and let's bring the past to life!"

Eurich inserted the slide into the opening at the base of the projector and waited.

"Thank you! One moment while we process the DNA…Ah! I see you have a *Cuculus canorus*. Fascinating bird. They were a zygodactyl species. Your specimen is a female. Would you like more interesting facts on your animal?"

"No. Just show me the bird already."

"Alright! Let's get started." Curios' image disappeared and after a few seconds another image started to take shape one strand at a time. The end result was a rather bland and unimpressive brown bird with a white chest striped with more brown.

"Bunch of dip," Eurich muttered as he returned the Holovid to its place and went to eat supper.

A dippin' week. That's how long he'd been staring at this stupid cuckoo bird. He knew everything there was to know about the Common Cuckoo. And he wasn't all that impressed. He was helping his mom bathe his brother in the kitchen sink when the idea came to him. The Replicator. Normally used to produce food and water in a society strapped for precious resources, the Replicator was an amazing machine. A small gelatinous cube was dropped into the slot and a few minutes later, four servings of water and protein mash came out the other end. It could work…

"I said to hold him, Rich!" his mom insisted, bringing him out of his mental daze.

"Sorry mom," he mumbled tightening his grip on his squirmy brother, but his eyes drifted to the Replicator.

Later that night when the house was quiet and everyone asleep, Eurich crept into the kitchen and stole the Replicator from its place on the kitchen counter. Then he snatched his dad's tool kit and barricaded himself in his bedroom, getting right to work. About an hour before dawn he'd finished his modifications and surveyed his contraption with an expert eye.

"Perfect," he mumbled to himself and switched on the power.

"Attention," said the Holovid immediately, "Unauthorized hardware configuration detected. Please power down and contact Customer Service."

"Service this." Eurich said as he accessed his eye screen. His fingers moved over the invisible keys more deftly than his father and in a few seconds he grunted in satisfaction.

"Administrator Override approved. Thank you."

"No. Thank *you*." Eurich slipped the DNA sample slide into the Replicator and turned on the machines. The Replicator hummed and clicked longer than usual as it processed the DNA sample. After a few minutes, the Holovid clicked on and began building a 3D image one pixel at a time. The whole process took much longer than Eurich had patience for, but the end result caught his breath. As the final pixel was placed on the new image, it sprang to life and the first Common Cuckoo was born into the world in over 200 years. It chirped and fluttered its wings, trying to take flight.

Eurich squealed in surprise and delight and snatched the bird before it could fly off. "I'll name you Margora. You like that?" He did. It was his mother's name.

The bird chirped.

"Shhh, Margora. Nobody can know you're here. I'll bring you some food later." He gingerly placed it in a glass container in the drawers beneath his bed and then hurried to dismantle his contraption so the Replicator would be ready for the family's breakfast portions.

∞

"Eurich, come here."

Eurich sat down in front of his father who was busy on his eye screen. "What is it, dad?"

"Mom says you've been helping out with Danich lately."

"Yeah…"

"I'm proud of you for helping. 'Drones are social not individual,'" he recited. "I have something for you." Though he was looking right at him, Eurich knew his father wasn't actually looking at him but at the computer screen projecting inside his eyeball. "It's on the table. Why don't you go and get it."

On the table sat another box, identical to the one that Eurich had received the week before. "Blazin! Thanks dad!" He ripped into the package quicker than the first and held aloft his new slide. It read: *Androctonus crassicauda.*
"Androc…tonus…Crass…eye…cauda…"

"A scorpion," said his dad. "A nasty one."

"Blazin! I'm going to go try it out! You wanna come check it out with me?" he asked with a tone of childlike hopefulness in his voice.

"I'd love to son. I really would. But we're down three hundred points in the Chinese market. And you know what HQ says."

"The only good drone is a profitable drone," they chimed in a monotonous unison.

"That's right," said his father. "Now run along. I need to get this done before dinner."

"*Androctonus crassicauda,* or the Arabian Fat-tail scorpion, was one of the most deadly species of scorpion in the world until its extinction in twenty-two twenty-two," the Holovid explained. "Though small, it was known to kill a man with one sting."

"Blazin," breathed Eurich, almost reverently. He'd spent most of the night absorbing all the information the Holovid had on his sample, which was another female. When he'd exhausted the Holovid's encyclopedia entry he switched it off and checked on his cuckoo.

It fluttered helplessly against the container's ceiling as Eurich pulled the drawer out. He'd snuck some grass and leaves in so it could build a nest and had scrounged up a few cockroaches for it to eat. Despite all this, it still looked sad and sickly.

"What's wrong, Margora? Do you want me to make you a friend? I bet you'd like a friend, wouldn't you?"

The cuckoo chirped pathetically and Eurich ran into the kitchen, returning with the Replicator. Rigging the machines didn't take half the time it took him the first time. Within 90 minutes he'd created a scorpion which he placed in his other container under his bed.

"Isn't it awesome, Marge?" he asked the cuckoo. "I made it just like I made you!"

It was while he was admiring his creations that his ultimate idea came to him. He took both slides, putting one on top of the other, slid them into the machine and turned it on.

Pixels flew from the hologram machine, building Eurich's new creation. It started out like a bird. With two bird legs and a beak and wings and feathers. But the body soon elongated, adding six more legs, and pinchers sprang from its chest. The tail appeared just as the Fat Tail scorpion's: black and menacing with a wicked stinger on the end of it.

"Blazin," breathed the boy, "This is so dippin awesome!"

When the process finished, the hybrid let out a piercing shriek and tried to take flight, only to fall to the ground in a clumsy heap.

"Where you think you're going, you squirrelly monster?" Eurich corralled it into the same container as his scorpion. "That's what I'll call you. Squirrelly," he informed it as he put the container back in his drawer and slid it under his bed. "You guys sleep tight. I'll see you in the morning."

The next morning, Eurich's room stank like bird shit. Margora had literally pooped in every square inch of her cage overnight. The smell wafted through the air holes in the container. His mom would kill him if she found out. He'd have to clean it up after Academy today. But until then…he opened his window a crack to let the smell out.

"Eurich! Let's go! You're going to be late!" his mom called from the living room.

"Coming!" he yelled back and took one last look at his creations.

Squirrelly had eaten the scorpion during the night. Her venomous tail clicked against the plastic lid of the container trying to sting Eurich.

"Squirrelly! Be nice! And quit scaring Margora!"

"Eurich!!"

"I'll see you guys after Academy." The boy slid the drawer under his bed and left for school.

"Shut up you stupid homie, you did not!" accused Davich, the Academy's bully. He had made it a point to make Eurich's life a living nightmare because he lived at home instead of in the barracks like most of the other children.

"I did so! I made a monster! I named it Squirrelly!"

"I said shut up!" Davich shoved Eurich to the ground, causing his other classmates to laugh. "You still have something to say about monsters?"

"Yes! And I'm going to let her loose on you!"

Davich kicked his prey in the gut and in the back a few times. "How bout now? How bout now!!" The bully yelled and the children gathered cheered him on until the bell rang, breaking up the crowd.

"Stupid human," Davich said with one final kick, then left for class.

Eurich climbed to his feet grumbling, "I did make a monster, you idiot."

∞

Dance opened the door to his big brother's room, ignoring the "Keep OUT DAN!!" sign written in bold red ink. It was his most favorite place in the world. It was a toddler's paradise, full of wondrous sights and nifty gadgets to play with. He went right for the drawer under the bed. Even at two, Danich knew that was where Eurich kept his best treasures. He pulled it out and wrinkled his nose at the smell. Something was squawking in one of the compartments. Dan couldn't see inside because it was all smeared with white. So he unclasped the lid and opened it.

Margora the cuckoo exploded into the air in a flutter of feathers and feces. She made right for the window and escaped through the opening.

Dan watched the entire process in awe and wonder. He'd only seen birds a dozen times in his life. What was his brother doing with one? The question was forgotten as soon as he laid eyes on the other compartment. Inside it was a monster. A real monster! It was easily the most hideous thing Danich had ever seen, even in the nightmares he remembered. Its tail clacked against the lid of the compartment and the pinchers on its chest opened and closed. He had to touch it! He opened the lid and the creature scurried up his arm. He giggled at the feeling. It crawled over his shoulder and down his back.

"That tickles," he giggled and then screamed as the burning pain filled his body.

∞

"I'm sorry Mrs. Dunhill. We really don't know what to do for your son." The doctor fidgeted with the clipboard ashamedly as he spoke.

"What do you mean you can't help him?" Marge was in hysterics. She was a rarity. In an age where children were raised by corporate institutions, she had chosen to keep her sons at home. This opened their family up to ridicule, not to mention internal conflict. She and Edrich had argued about it almost constantly for the first 2 years of Eurich's life.

It's stupid, Margora! The only good drone is a profitable drone! That's why we send our children off. So they can grow up to be profitable drones and we can drone on with our own profit making. It's just what people do.

To the graces with what people do! She'd insisted. *He's my baby. Mine. I love him and I'm not shipping him off to be raised by some damn corporation.*

Careful what you say, Edrich had warned her with a cautious glance at the televid. Its built-in camera was always watching, always listening.

Let them hear me. I LOVE MY FAMILY!! She yelled. *And I don't care how stupid or crazy that sounds!*

Alright, fine. You want to raise a house full of homies, that's on you. But if your production drops and you get reassigned, don't say I didn't warn you. He then turned back to his eye screen and that's the last she'd heard of it.

But she hadn't cared about all of that. Let people talk. Let them snicker and gossip. Humanity had survived with family units for tens of thousands of years. It was only in the past few centuries that parents started giving up their rights to their children so they could focus more on work. But something about it was unnatural. She knew that for certain once she'd laid eyes on her first born son.

The doctor cleared his throat snapping Marge from her reverie. "The tests. They don't make sense. We haven't seen anything like it, well, ever, to be honest. There are almost no diseases that modern medicine can't cure. Cancer. AIDS. Heart Disease. You name the affliction, it can be fixed. But this…this isn't a disease."

"Then what is it?"

"That's what's puzzling. The tests, and we've run them five times, they say it's a venom."

"Venom? From what?"

"A type of scorpion extinct for over 300 years."

"How is that possible?"

"That's what we wanted to ask you. Does anyone in your family have a living Arabian Fat Tail scorpion?"

Marge was dumbfounded. It was the most absurd thing she'd ever heard. Her son was dying beside her and this doctor (and she used the term loosely) was babbling on about extinct arachnids! "Are you serious?"

"Yes, ma'am. We are. As you know, the Hospital works closely with HQ. We could have an anti-venom in a day."

"Well, we don't have any dead scorpions."

"Oh well," sighed the doctor, "Not that it would likely do any good. Anti-venom was hard to come by during the scorpion's time. But we've come so far since then so I hoped…No matter. With the poison reacting abnormally like it is there probably isn't much time."

"Abnormal? What are you talking about?"

"It's not acting like venom should. It's not affecting his neurological functions. It's attached itself to Danich's internal organs. It's eating him from the inside out. At the rate it's going,

Danich will be dead within two hours. I'm sorry." The doctor exited, leaving Marge sobbing into the pillow next to her son's head.

∞

"Squirrelly! Where are you?!" Eurich called as he tore his room apart. Stupid Dan! He wasn't even supposed to be in his room, that's what the sign was for, by all the Graces! It wasn't his fault if his stupid baby brother didn't read the sign and got hurt because of it.

"Signs point the way to success," he mumbled the slogan while digging through his closet.

Not only was Squirrelly missing, Margora was too. He figured the cuckoo had flown out the window, but the hybrid couldn't fly. Certainly not. It was then he caught midair movement out of the corner of his eye, but when he turned to look it was gone.

"Oh dip," he whispered.

∞

"No. Oh no." Edrich's fingers stopped in mid-type. "I'll get Rich and we'll be right down…Are you sure?…O.K. We'll see you when you get home." The call ended and Eddie sighed hugely and ran his fingers through his hair. "Eurich! Come here please!"

His son appeared flushed and out of breath.

"What have you been doing in there?"

"Pushups," the boy lied.

"Uh huh." It was this kind of thing that could've been avoided if Marge had chosen to send the boy to the Academy. But she refused, much to Eddie's annoyance. Raising kids wasn't worth the time and effort. They were a constant annoyance, always underfoot. There were trained parenting professionals to handle children now. He could use one right now. Especially when talking about the news he just got. "I have some news about your brother, Danich."

"I know Dan's my brother, dad. Is he better? Is he coming home soon? The doctors fixed him up real good I bet. That's what doctors do. They fix things."

Eddie sighed and ran his fingers through his hair again. "No. He's not better, son. And he's not coming home. He…he passed into the Graces a few minutes ago."

Eurich's eyes widened as he shook his head. "No! No! No, no, no! Stupid monster! Stupid!" He started beating his head with his tiny, meaty fists until he was restrained by his father. Once his rage was spent, he collapsed into Edrich, sobbing apologies.

"It's ok," Eddie soothed his son, albeit awkwardly. His embrace was stiff and his words without emotion. "It's not your fault."

"Yes it is, dad! I'm a dippin' pisser!"

"Language!"

"Who gives a dip about my language? It's my fault Dan is dead!" He then unburdened himself of his story.

Eddie was quiet for a while after his son's confession.

"Dad? Are you ok?"

"Yes. I, well, I don't know what to say." He looked at the televid in the wall and back at his son with apprehension in his eyes. "Look, what you just told me, you can't tell anyone else. Ever. You understand?"

"Why not?"

"Because if you do and HQ hears about it, your mom will be upset. She's been through enough. We don't want to upset her any more than she already is, do we?"

"No."

"Good then. I'll make you up a bed on the couch. You get some rest and I'll go find Squirrelly."

"Dad no!" pleaded Eurich. "She's evil! And I think she can fly now!" He clutched his dad tightly.

"Stay here, I'll be alright," said Eddie as he pried his son off and tucked him beneath the blanket on the couch. "I'll handle it."

He grabbed the autobroom from the kitchen and burst through Eurich's bedroom door like an ungainly ninja swinging the broom handle like a sword. Once inside, he slammed the door behind him.

"Squirrelly! Here girl!" He whistled, hoping to draw out the beast.

It didn't work.

"Squirrelly," he called again as he inspected the room carefully.

He checked under the bed.

Nothing.

He looked behind everything on the shelf and almost died of fright when the Holovid accidentally turned on displaying a holographic image of the mutation. He had a good laugh and wiped the sweat from his brow before continuing the search.

He dumped out the laundry bin and sifted through the clothes with the broom handle.

They were clean. No hybrid bird-scorpion to be found.

He returned the clothes to the hamper and heard a chime inside his ear that notified him of an email. Thinking it could be from Marge, he switched on his eye screen and started scrolling through them. He'd actually missed fifteen emails since Eurich's confession. His fingers typed in the air and he wandered over to the window, staring outside as he worked. He felt something land on his shoulder followed quickly by a burning pain in his back.

"Of course. The lip above the window," he mumbled and then collapsed.

Eurich heard the thud.

"Dad?" he called in a trembling voice and peeked over the back of the couch. "Dad? What's going on?"

No answer.

He slid off the couch and crept slowly toward his room and eased the door open. "Dad?" he whispered loudly.

"Rich…don't…it's…"

"Dad!" Eurich threw open the door and rushed to where his father lay. "Oh no! Not you too! I'm sorry! I'm so sorry!"

Eddie's eyes flickered open and met his son's gaze for the first time. "Such a beautiful boy," he coughed. "How could I not see? So much wasted time…Don't…tell them anything…son…only good drone…don't tell them. Promise me!"

"I promise, dad. Please don't die. Please don't! I love you!"

"Good boy." He patted his son's cheek. "I…I called 911. Be a good boy and let them in. I love…" he mumbled and then went limp.

Eurich rushed to unlock the door for the EMS and stopped dead in his tracks. On the counter that separated the kitchen from the living room, Squirrelly perched ready to attack. The pinchers protruding from her chest clacked and she fluttered her wings, squawking at her creator.

"You dumb monster!" said the boy as he eased into the kitchen. "You killed everybody! I wish I never made you!"

In response, the chimera attacked. It flew at Eurich, a deadly mass of exoskeleton and feathers. He desperately grabbed for something to defend himself with and came up with his dad's dirty coffee mug. He slung it at the creature with all his might. Luck was with him. The mug struck Squirrelly in midair sending her careening into the sink.

The mutant flopped around trying to right itself for another attack. Eurich didn't waste any time. He grabbed the Replicator off the counter next to the sink and brought it down on his creation again and again screaming curses at it the entire time. When he was done, all that remained of Squirrelly was a gooey mass of feathers.

"Dippin pisser!" he screamed at the remains and then there was a loud knock on the door.

"This is EMS! Open the door!"

Eurich complied, sobbing with joy. Everything would be alright now.

Three days later Eurich sat with his mother beside his father's hospital bed. The doctor had been able to synthesize an anti-venom from Squirrelly's remains, but the poison had already done extensive damage to Edrich's internal organs.

"He's in a coma now," the doctor had explained. "And probably will be for a very long time."

Marge hadn't left her husband's side, much to Eurich's dismay. And as boredom claimed him yet again, he tried to persuade his mom to leave.

"C'mon mom! We'll just go down to the caf. I hear their fish sticks are blazin'!"

"No." answered Marge hollowly. "What if your father wakes up while we're gone?"

"Then he'll be awake when we get back. C'mon, please! Can't we just go out for a little bit?"

"I said no."

Their argument was interrupted by a soft rapping on the door that preceded the entrance of a very well dressed man with oily hair and a thin mustache.

"Mrs. Dunhill, I take it? And you must be Eurich. I'm Maxwell from HQ."

"What do you want?" asked Marge.

"I'm here with an exciting opportunity for Eurich."

"What kind of opportunity?" said the boy, perking up.

"I'm offering you a place at Academy Elite for special boys and girls like you."

"Academy Elite?" interrupted Marge. "That's for high preforming students. I have trouble keeping Rich at median."

"Yes, well, studies have shown that most homies preform lower in academics than their corporate ward peers. Be that as it may, we aren't interested in Eurich's academic performance, per se. Although that will improve, won't it young man?" Maxwell chided good naturally

"Then what are you interested in my son for?" Marge didn't trust this drone from HQ. Drones like him didn't show up unless HQ wanted something and planned to take it one way or another.

"He's a very smart young man."

"I'm not smart," Insisted Eurich

"Oh, we beg to differ. What you did with the Replicator was, how should I put this? It was inspiring, Eurich."

"I didn't do nothing with the Replicator," said Eurich, remembering the promise to his father.

"That's not what you told your mates at the Academy, now is it? And it's not what you told your father last night."

Eurich flushed and looked at his mom.

"What did you do with the Replicator?" Marge asked sharply.

"Nothing! I promise."

She didn't buy it. A mom can smell a lie a mile off. "It was you, wasn't it?"

The boy met his mom's gaze, tears falling unbidden. "I'm so sorry."

"It was you! They're dead because of you!" Marge couldn't take any more heartache. What was left of her sanity shattered and all she saw was red. She leapt at Eurich in a blind fury and turned her wrath on Maxwell when he tried to interfere.

Orderlies burst in almost immediately, restraining and sedating the grieving woman with powerful drugs.

"I'm so sorry, sir," said the doctor who came in after the commotion had died down. "I treated her son recently. She's been through a lot lately."

"So she has," said Maxwell, straightening his clothes. "Though her problems go far deeper than a mere family tragedy. Studies have shown that only the most unbalanced drones opt to raise homies. See that she gets the best, most extensive psychological treatment and reeducation the Hospital has to offer. HQ will pay for it."

"As you say," the doctor said and nodded to the orderlies who hauled the drugged woman out.

"My babies. Don't take my babies," Marge mumbled weakly, unable to resist.

"I'm sorry you had to see that, son," said Maxwell. "Now come along." He reached out his hand.

Eurich looked at his father lying comatose in the bed and ran his fingers through his hair. "He said he loved me. Do you know that?"

"Yes. We were watching. Don't worry about your dad, son. The doctors will make him well. Now shall we? Your new family and friends are waiting for you. Let's go home." He extended his hand again and this time Eurich took it.

∞

Outside, Margora, the cuckoo, took flight. True to her brood parasitic nature, she had laid eggs in a pigeon's nest (one of the few remaining species of bird) and now she longed to have the wind under her wings. She was free. Free of the invisible cage that the Manchild had imprisoned her in. Free of the terrifying presence of her abhorrent mutant kin. And her liberation was exhilarating. The cuckoo soared higher and higher the world of men fell away below the clouds and the winds bore her into the world anew.

The House

By

Reagan Thompson

There I was. Standing over the edge of the window, looking out in the distance, not knowing what awaited me. As I looked down, all I could see was black. Black waters violently crashing against the house, and with every crash, the house shook, causing me to lose my balance every time. A small, suicidal part of me wanted to let go and jump to my death. How bittersweet it would be to be able to let go of anything at any time... but that's the case, isn't it? I had the option to let myself go at any time I wanted, but I never had the inclination to do so until now. A wave of sudden realization overcame me, and I realized that we are all suicidal in some way. We're just too cowardly to admit it, but not me. I admit it. We have that option dangling in front of my face every day, a knife just lying in wait, waiting to be used. A bridge above rapid waters and razor-edged rocks appeared before us every day. Cars whizzing by, waiting to impact another brave soul. Strangers' hands in our vicinity, waiting to grasp and snap our necks. And there I was. Ready to let go. I looked down once again and saw my fate. I closed my eyes, took the plunge and waited for fate to take me.

     Then I awoke.
Heart beating…
Heart beating…

     This was the fourth time this week alone that I had woken up in a cold sweat, and I found myself in a puddle, sloshing about. I groaned as I could feel my body stick to the bed sheets as I slowly sat up and cursed silently to myself, "Fuck me." It was completely pitch black except for the moonlight gleaming through the window, and it was hitting particularly on a poster of a little boy fishing at a secluded pond. Every time I look at the poster, I get this feeling of freedom and the sense of being able to grasp it for myself as if I could reach into the poster and trade places with the little boy for I could truly live happily if I were him. And then I noticed the ominous red glow of my alarm clock, which read three zero zero in distinctive red numbers, although, on this particular night just like the other three, the glow was rather bright. It was rather curious and led my mind to wander with endless possibilities. My paranoia had been at an all-time high the past few nights. I didn't know why. I had my suspicions, but I still didn't know.

     3-0-5. Five minutes had passed, and I was still sitting in my puddle of sweat, being unable to move due to my persisting paranoia. There was no sound that had woken me up. There was nothing out of the ordinary that could have woken me up. Three one zero. Five more minutes had passed, and I knew that I needed to get out of bed. I swung my legs off the edge of the bed and stood up. The moon from my window right across from me immediately hit my face, and it seemed to draw me towards the window. I put my hand on the glass and felt a chilling sensation run up my arm all the way to every nerve ending in my body. It was a cool relief from the hot sweat puddle I had woken up in. The crystal, transparent glass brought me immediate relief and rid me of my paranoia.

I lived in the middle of nowhere with no surrounding neighbors due to my parents' lack of camaraderie, although we did live about a mile from this old, worn-down house, which was presented right in front of my bedroom window. But the house was much too far away to fully notice how old and broken down it was, which was how my parents described it to me. The first time I had taken notice of that house was when I was ten. I was outside playing with the tire swing that my father had built immediately after I was born, and it was the first time I had taken an interest in the house. I remember it just as if it were yesterday.

It was a glorious day; the sun was shining bright; there was a cool breeze blowing just enough to complement the heat coming from the sun. All was right in the world. As I swung higher and higher on the tire swing, an unfamiliar object started appearing in the corner of my eye, and my feet stopped the tire from swinging. I started walking towards the object not knowing what it was. As I walked closer and closer, I started to break out in a sprint, becoming excited about not knowing what this was and the adventure of finding out. As I became within spitting distance, I realized that it was a house. A two story wooden house, as old as time itself. The roof shingles had been either stripped away or degraded due to neglect. All that was left of the roof, were its wooden beams providing just a lonely frame. There was a small window near the cellar door, which led to the basement, I figured. The glass was insanely fogged up and was impossible to see through. And then my gaze went to this door with a long, rectangular window and a single doorknob, seeming to barely be hanging onto the door. This seemed as if it wasthe only way into the house so I started to reach for the doorknob, when all of a sudden, I heard a noise, which appeared to be very distinctive.

I froze.
My hand stopped reaching.
All of a sudden, I felt arms being wrapped around me, and I was instantly lifted off the ground with no struggle at all. As soon as my feet left contact with the ground, everything went black. The next thing I remember was waking up at three a.m. in a puddle of my own sweat. It was as if nothing had ever happened.

That was eight years ago; I am eighteen now, and I still wake up in a cold sweat at exactly three a.m. on random nights.

Ever since that traumatic night, I had an inhumane, burning obsession with that house, although, I could never seem to bring myself to go back. It was as if a fear-induced disease riddled my mind to no end, and I was stuck within the confines of my own room and my home. I rarely went outside ever since that night, and I was perfectly content with the situation I was in. I was safe and sound in my own home, and it seemed as if no one or nothing could ever persuade me to ever voluntarily escape, but as life would have it, I had spoken far too soon.

Once I awoke, it was impossible for me to sleep again, and I would not get any sleep until the following night at exactly ten p.m., which was another unusual routine of mine, so I bided my time by sitting at my desk, staring outside of the window, gazing at the night sky, dreaming of what might have been. Since we lived in the middle of nowhere, there were no lights in our vicinity to pollute the night sky. The stars shining brought me a sense of purity. In the quiet hours of the late night, I liked to write poetry as an escape from the pathetic life I led. It was the only thing left that was mine and mine alone, and I held a special regard for it in my heart. The theme of all my poems was inspired by my feelings of helplessness and loneliness…

> *Trapped behind the window*
> *Of a 47-4*
> *Always flying high*
> *Racing the race*
> *Never winning*
> *But never wanting to die*
>
> *Is it all just a dream?*
> *Is there no escaping the beam?*
> *Balancing world's pain*
> *But really, who's to blame*
>
> *Just like Cain*

As I was writing all of my dark thoughts of utter loneliness, something caught my eye outside of the window as if a light was flickering. At first I had thought that it was just our porch light flickering below me. I paid no attention to it and continued writing. Then it happened again. But as soon as I looked up, there was nothing that seemed to be out of the ordinary. Just pitch black darkness with the gleam of the moon that shone onto the tall grass in our backyard with the tire swing slowly swinging in and out of the light from the steady wind. Again, I decided to brush it off as if my mind had been playing tricks on me due to the late hours of the night, and at this moment, I looked over to my alarm clock, which was beside my bed, and it reads 3-3-0. Twenty minutes had passed since I awoke, but it had felt like longer. Time was never a clear concept to me. I spent most of my time just sulking around my room or wandering around our house. I thought I was losing my sanity, so I decided to put my pen and paper down to pace back and forth, which proved to be a total mind cleanser. I did so quietly to make sure I wasn't making a racket due to the chance I might awake my parents.

Fucking relax...

I took a glance at my poster of the little boy and pretended I was in his place for a while, and that calmed me down quickly but not for long. When I looked around at the window, there was a light in the distance flickering. And it was at that moment that I knew my mind wasn't playing tricks on me. I instantly ducked under my desk. I was having heart palpitations, and I kept cursing over and over, "Jesus fucking Christ. Fuck. Fuck." I took a second to recollect myself, and then I peered over my desk just enough to get a view of the window and the house.

The light was off. I was flummoxed beyond belief, but decided to brush it off. I was sleep-deprived, so that was my excuse. I calmed myself to a point where I had accepted that there was a slight possibility of me becoming clinically insane.

To me, there were only two acceptable forms of insanity, no matter what anyone else thought. I would not accept any other forms. The first form is normal insanity, and this the most common form of the two.
Normal insanity is when everything in the world didn't necessarily make sense to your diseased mind, and there wasn't anything you could do about it. But, see, the thing is that you never really know. You just are. There can be a point in your life where you begin to notice it. Your insanity. Once you notice, there's no turning back. You know the truth. And that is enough to drive you insane. You become clinically insane.
Clinical insanity is when every drive, every power and every aspect of your human spirit just broke down and completely gave up, but the thing was that you were fully aware and in your right state-of-mind, in a disturbing way, that you were insane. Those are the two forms, and everything else is somewhat arbitrary. I was the latter of the two. I was clinically insane. I knew that to be true, and to me, it was the only sure and pure thought I had thus far in my eighteen years of living.

I got up and sat down at my seat. I picked up the pen and started to write random words, hoping it would attempt to keep my mind sane for the time being, but I already knew. I knew that my mind was past the line between sanity and insanity. I looked behind me, at the red glow of the clock, which seemed to be glowing even brighter, as if it were becoming brighter as every minute passed. The time read 4-0-0. Thirty minutes had passed.

The moon was high in the sky, and it moved its gaze from the tire swing to the house. As soon as I set sights in the direction of the house, which appeared as invisible due to the thick blackness of the night. The moon's glow barely reached the house for it only shone on the field between. There wasn't anything right about the atmosphere, and there wasn't anything out of the ordinary. But nothing sat right with me. And then I saw it.

A figure.

It was walking towards me.

I saw it as clear as day, or in this case, as clear as the moon allowed it. The figure had the apparent shape of a man. I could not make out who or what it was. The only thought that crossed my mind was to run, but I could not move. My feet were glued to the ground, and my gaze never broke the figure's movements; my eyes refused to let go. I was in a dormant state. The figure stopped for a short while, and I could feel its demonic energy drawing me in.

Then the figure picked up its pace. I immediately broke my gaze and sprinted out of my room, down the stairs and into my parents' bedroom only to find that it was empty. They were nowhere to be found, nor was their bed slept in. The golden brown sheets and comforter on the bed were fitted perfectly. Almost too perfectly. It had seemed as if no one had been in it for a long while. I walked over to their drawers, and started opening them all, and to my astonishment, they were all empty. No clothes. No shirts. No pants. No socks. No, nothing. I backed away slowly and ran to the room next door, which was my father's office. It was normally filled with too many books to name on his bookshelf, documents scattered all over his desk next to his computer and his cigar box always filled up to the brim with his exquisite cigars, as he called them. But when I entered the room, nothing was the same as it was the day before or the week before, but it was just as well that everything was exactly the same. The atmosphere was completely off in the room just as it was in the bedroom. His desk occupied all of his papers he needed for work, and it was in the exact same order as it always had been. The cigar box was filled up to the brim, but there wasn't that sweet aroma of smoke in the air, along with the intimidating ambience of intelligence. Both were lacking. The bookshelf was stocked with books he collected throughout the years, and one of them caught my eye. *History of Children.* An ominous mood started to fill me up.

What in the fuck? I thought to myself.

I scoured the room for something that would give me a clue of the whereabouts of my father and my mother but to no avail. My heart was completely broken. I was lost, and I had no idea what was occurring inside of my own house. It was at that moment I had the sudden realization that the figure was still out there, and it was coming.

I heard a door slowly creak open.
It was here.
Heart beating...
Heart beating...

I ran as fast as I could up the stairs to my room and slammed the door. It was coming for me, and it was going to kill me. I was absolutely sure of that.

"Don't be afraid," the figure said. The voice came from downstairs. My ears felt as if they were being slowly tortured with a knife buried deep down inside and slowly turning until I bled to death just before begging to die. The voice pulsated an extreme noise of static that was simultaneously static-like and clear. It was the strangest, yet the most compelling thing I had ever heard. For some reason, the voice was music to my ears, although it was torture.

Imagine being so deeply in love that it tears away at your every reason to live and your every reason to wake up in the morning. Imagine being so deeply in love that it takes away your very bane of existence and tears away at your humanity until there is nothing except the purest parts of your soul hanging on for dear life, and then the next morning, it starts all over again.

That's what the voice felt like. Toxic, yet beautiful, but I knew in the deepest pits of my insanity-riddled mind that I needed to escape, and the window was my only chance. "Let me see that beautiful face. Let me see your face." The voice was coming up the stairs. I opened the window and crept on the roof. The voice was drawing closer and closer, causing me to regret every step I was taking. I took a deep breath and jumped. The instant I hit the ground, immediate regret filled me up to from head to toe. I felt a crack in my leg, and I screamed in agonizing pain. Everything went black for an instant, and then I came to. The tall grass surrounded me as I looked up at the roof from where I jumped and suffered only a broken leg. I was in unbearable, throbbing pain and could not get up until I just saw it. It was unrecognizable due to the darkness consuming its face. It was standing over me on the rooftop, looking straight into my soul. I felt as if it could peer into and open up all the darkness inside of me and unlock it free. It did not move nor did I. With all of my strength, I broke my gaze and forced my limp body to get up and start running as fast as I could, which deemed almost impossible. I ran and I ran and I ran as fast as physically possible without looking back, because I knew that once I looked back, that was going to be it for me. That would have been the end of my pathetic excuse of a life of loneliness and regret. I could see the house in the distance, and to my shock, the light was on.

I went into the house. As I came up against the door, grimacing in pain, I hesitated for a second and began to think to myself, *What if I actually die? That would be horrible.* I laughed and walked in.

I opened the door. As the door slowly opened, I was welcomed with absolutely nothing except darkness. The kind of darkness that I felt when the figure peered into my soul. I immediately slammed the door shut, locked it, and then began to feel my way around the room, trying to get a hold of another door that led farther and farther away from the figure. I was fumbling around in the dark for God knows how much time. I found it. There was a door, and I could feel the creases in it but no doorknob. In anger, I kicked down the door only to find myself thrown into more darkness and despair. The gleam of the moon shone through the window of the outside door into the house and provided very little light. I could only make out a few feet in front of me, and there were stairs that led to what I had assumed was the basement. I had no other choice except to descend down the stairs. It was coming for me. As I raised my hands in order to shield me from what might be in my way, I could not see them. It was as if I was drowning in a sea deeper and deeper to the bottom. I felt as though I could not breathe. I was suffocating. The air felt excruciatingly musty and overcame me like darkness.

This was not a means to an end, but a means to a beginning.

My hands were sliding frantically all over the walls, and then I felt a beacon of hope blossom inside of me. There it was. I ran my fingers over the light switch, but there was nothing that I could see. No light had turned on, but in the corner of my eye, I could make out such a dim light. It was so dim that I could hardly see the area around it. I slowly made my way across the room as I had gotten to the bottom of the stairs, making sure I didn't trip across anything for it was still a blanket of darkness. Everything was silent. Too silent. The atmosphere was too eerie, and when I finally came within spitting distance of the light, my heart instantly dropped.

The dim light was a small lamp on a wooden table on the far side of the room opposite of the stairs. It was just a lamp all by its lonesome and aside from it was a small, golden brown chest with worn down leather straps. The straps weren't fastened. There was no lock, which made me assume that nothing inside of it was meant to be private or so I thought. As a reflex, I looked behind me, but I could barely see anything, even with the glow of the dimly lit lamp. There was the unsettling thought of the figure still being out there, not knowing whether it was in the house or not, because my sense of sound was distracted by my surroundings. It was too quiet in that room. I could hear my own heartbeat.

Heart beating...
Heart beating...

I reached for the box with my clammy hands and quickly opened it. As I looked inside, I found newspaper clippings filled with reports of kids missing. The year on the newspapers was 1985.

That was eighteen years ago. I was confused. I started looking
through them one by one.

    Bobby Brown
    Christina Gardner
    Oliver Scott
    Serena Faulkner

    I had no idea who those people were. As I kept on reading,
my body went into shock. My heart stopped. I came across a name
I knew very well.

    My own.
    Charles Davenport.

SOPHIE

By

David Thomas

If it had been summer things might have turned out differently. But it wasn't summer, it was winter, and the coldest one any of the old folks could remember. At thirteen Neil didn't have the memories to say for sure, but it *was* cold, to that he *could* attest.

So, it was winter when the Spellman's waited for the birth of their second child, at least that was the plan. It was also the same plan Neil had watched his parents put into motion twice since he was born and both of those times his mother had miscarried. Hopes were running high this time though as his mother had carried his new brother or sister almost to full term with no problems.

Yes, this time would be different, Neil was sure of it.

He wanted to help with the birth. And why not? He was old enough and had helped his pop with the births of every type of animal on the farm and he couldn't see why his mom should be any different.

His pop just kept telling him that they would talk about it, but they never seemed to.

His mom still handled the cooking and wash, but he had taken to helping out with the cleaning after spending the day in the fields with his pop.

And the whole time he was waiting…waiting for the baby.

The next day dawned gray and snowy and Neil trudged around doing the endless chores that it took to keep a farm running. By the time he slogged through the snow to the house he could hear his mom.

Hear his mom screaming.

He began to run at that sound. He ran through the kitchen forgetting to pull his boots off, slipped and fell on the hardwood floor in the living room before hurtling himself through the door of his parents room.

His blundering entrance startled his pop who was between his mother's legs; arms red with blood.

"What can I do pop?"

His pop turned back to the awful looking mess in front of him;

"Go on boy, there ain't nothin' you can do now."

When he hesitated, he said softly over his shoulder;

"Go on now. Go to your room."

After a few hours he heard the door and looked out the window, outside his father carried a small bundle and placed it in among the firewood in the wood box.

∞

That night was the first night he heard his sister Sophie calling him…

…It was a dream of course, what else could it be? And what did it mean when she said he was the only one who could help them all? Who was "them all"?

The next day got back to normal and was spent doing chores as usual, making up for his mother who was still in bed. At one point he overheard his parents talking, his pop telling his unusually quiet mother that when the thaw came, he would bury the baby with the others, until then the cold would keep the body from rotting.

He could hear his mother's soft sobs.

His pop seemed so unfeeling about the whole thing, but then again, he'd been thru it before, so maybe you get used to these things when you're a grown up. That was the thought that he had as he fell asleep.

That night his sister spoke to him again and told Neil he was the only one who could help all his siblings. He woke thinking about that; he didn't have any brothers and sisters, not really. Not even the one who told him that, but at least now he knew who "them all" was supposed to be. It made no more sense, but he felt he knew something more now, he just didn't know what to do with the information.

The work that day was the same as the day before and the day before that except for one thing; the ravens.

He heard them all at once. He had realized that one or two ravens cawing and upset was bothersome at best, but that hundreds of them was horrible. Neil figured it had to be hundreds of them because they were all in the oak tree and their numbers were enough that the limbs were weighted down and the tree itself deformed out of shape by their feathery bodies.

As one they stopped cawing and the silence was even worse. After what seemed to Neil to be forever, but must have just been a few minutes they took flight in a wave that he had never seen ravens do. They flew in an almost straight line (though in several places they were at least twenty wide). They flew down and toward the wood box that held Sophie's small body, most managing to peel off at the last second, but more than a few couldn't control their dive and slammed into the box and the firewood around it, falling, broken and in most cases dead.

Neil stood stunned looking at the aftermath wondering what it could mean.

∞

Exhausted, he'd fallen into bed and asleep quickly only to wake to the voice of his baby sister. This time, she said, she wanted to see him. She wanted him to come outside to her. Barefoot he padded outside and opened the wood box, inside, he found the bundled up bodies and gently picked it up and looked at the tiny body.

He couldn't figure out how she could talk to him. He could tell just looking at her that she was not alive (any idiot could) and even if she were she was too young to be able to talk. But as he held her lifeless body, she *did* speak.

She spoke to him on the same subject she had the two previous nights but he still didn't understand. He still didn't understand what Sophie could mean about him being the only person who could help her and their other two siblings. They were all dead, even he knew that and he wasn't even smart enough to go to the school some of the other kids in the area went to. Hell, two weren't just dead, they were buried in the backfield somewhere. She was sure of it though, that he could help them. He was getting dizzy and sick to his stomach from the queer buzzing feeling in his head where he heard a Sophie's voice, it was like there were millions of bees in his brain.

He put Sophie back among the cordwood and stumbled back inside and slept again, only waking when he heard his pop yelling for him from the kitchen. He hurriedly dressed and ran, and as he entered the room, he felt a leather strap across his back so unexpectedly, it drove him to his knees on the dirty linoleum. Still stunned another blow landed across his shoulders and he began to cry. Lord knows he didn't want to but he couldn't stop himself.

"What was you doing in the wooden box?"

"I...I wasn't pop."

Whap!

"Don't lie to me! I didn't accuse if you was there because I already know you was. I axed *what* was ya doin' there?"

"I don't...don't know..."

Whap!

It came down a fourth time.

"Ya got no bidness in there so don't be goin' out there agin!"

"Yes...yes sir. I...I ..." tears flooded his face then shamefully.

"I, I, I, what boy?" his pop mocked him.

"I won't go out there pop. I promise."

"Git off tha floor then, an go an do yer chores!"

Neil scrabbled to his feet and flew out of the back door towards the barn without even a look over at the wooden box.

Somehow he had made it through the day and that night he ate alone because his mother was still abed and his pop was gone until morning taking some stock to market. Neil limped to his bed and lay on it on his stomach still sore from the earlier strapping and fell asleep.

∞

Again, Sophie's voice woke him, but this time he tried to answer her wondering if she could hear him the way he heard her. He told her he couldn't come and what their pop had done that morning when he found out he had been visiting her. Sophie said she knew all of that, but if he was to help them it *had* to be tonight. It could not wait.

Reluctantly Neil got dressed and slunk as softly as he could outside and removed Sophie gently from the wooden box.

"We have to get our brothers Neil."

"Brothers?"

"Yes, our brothers."

He thought about all the times he had wished for a little brother to play with (and maybe be able to blame on things sometimes).

As if he'd spoken aloud Sophie answered him;

"You do *have a brother. You have two brothers* and *a sister if you would just help us Neil."*

"But you're all in heaven now, there's nothing I can do to help sis."

The buzzing in his head changed slightly (like a car radio going through a tunnel and on the other side for a second it picks up some other station). Now, instead of words Neil saw pictures and understood suddenly what he needed to do to help them.

"I don't know where our brothers are though."

"Just listen Neil, they have been trying to talk to you too, and you just weren't listening."

He screwed his eyes up tight and listened as hard as he could and concentrated;

"I hear them!" he said excitedly.

He found the spot of the two little unmarked graves and placing Sophie on the dew damp grass he dug them up with his hands. By the time he was done Neil's hands were numb from the cold, which he was grateful for because the frost hardened ground had torn his fingers up pretty good.

Having done what the pictures showed him, he found his way to bed and sleep.

When Mr. Spellman arrived home around four in the morning he removed his boots on the porch as much not to track mud in the house (for which he would catch hell) as to not wake his wife up, she'd had it hard the last few days and needed her sleep. But coming in he saw that at least that last was a wasted precaution as he saw a light spilling from the doorway of the room he shared with his wife. Still treading softly in case she had just gone to sleep with the light on he went through the door and screamed.

Never in his life, including his time in the war, had he screamed like this. He ran to his wife trying to grab the phone at the same time dropping it with a clang of the bell inside of it. He took one more look at his wife and slowly picked up the phone and called for an ambulance.

The sheriff arrived first and had to pull Mr. Spellman off of his son because he knew without a doubt that he intended to kill the boy. When he wouldn't calm down, he finally had a deputy place Mr. Spellman in the back of a cruiser so he could find out what in the hell had gone on in this house. He had a grim feeling that the story was going to have to come from the boy and he was determined to hear it.

Though he seemed almost comatose the boy would talk if you asked questions and finally he hit on the right one and the boy started talking a mile a minute and now, thought the sheriff, is when I hear what happened here.

The boy explained about the birth and how his sister (Sophie, he called her) had begun talking to him in the middle of the night. All about her and his two other dead brothers and how they needed his help for something.

"What did they need you to help them with son?"

But now asking questions was pointless the boy was on a roll and he would get to it when he got to it. He told about the night that was just ending out the windows with the rising of the sun and that's when he said it;

"I had to put them back."

"What do you mean son? Put them back?"

"I tried to put them back the way they come out." At this a small, confused frown appeared on his face, the first sign of emotion the sheriff had seen so far.

When he said this the sheriff shivered without meaning to remembering his first look at the woman in the bedroom. Now at least he knew what the two shriveled black sticks had been that he saw protruding from the woman's vagina.

Repulsed as he was, he had to hear the whole tale so he made the boy go on…

"Well, they wouldn't fit that way, I only barely got one of my brothers in there, so I figured they come out of belly and the way out is full…" here he shrugged so matter-of-factly that the sheriff understood why the boy's father had been trying to kill him, "…so I got a knife out of the kitchen and put my other brother and Sophie directly into her belly."

The sheriff thought for the first time in thirty years on the force that he might puke but he fought it. The boy was *so* calm about it. He still had to know one more thing though.

"Why? Why son? What did you think you were doing?"

"I was helping them."

"How in God's name did you think you were helping them?"

"Well, don't you see? Now she can finish them. Make Sophie and my brothers real so I'll have them to play with.

Esme's Piano

by

Blaise Ramsay

*"Every heart sings a song, incomplete, until another heart whispers back.
Those who wish to sing always find a song. At the touch of a lover,
everyone becomes a poet."*
— Plato

I'm not sure when all of the madness started. The day I stepped
off of the small plane bound for Washington to start a new duty
station as a ranger seemed like any other day.

It was raining. The cool spring wind added a slight hint of
humidity to the air despite the coolness. *This was going to be just like
any other transfer.* I thought. Little did I know I was about to be
proven wrong.

I was about to find myself in a world unlike any ever seen before. Some folks dream about it. Others claim to have seen it but rest assured the world written about in this memoir is real. They are real.

Before I begin, I feel the need to explain myself a bit. I'm not sure how I came to remember these words I'm about to share. For years the memories lay suppressed in the deepest recesses of the black hole of my mind.

It was only after I left that place they returned as though the place itself was the spell that bound them.

What I'm about to tell you may sound like a dream. It may sound made up. Something like the rambling of an old fool who spent too long at the bottom of the bottles of whiskey and Scotch beside his bedside.

I assure you, what you are about to read is real. It all happened what seems like so long ago but it happened nonetheless.

As I said, the day I stepped off of the plane bound to Washington didn't seem like anything special. It was raining and muggy; humid and sticky despite the coolness of the air.

I stood outside waiting for the sheriff's deputy sent to take me from Seattle to the new duty station I was assigned in the small town of Darrington, It wasn't too far away - about an hour's ride.

He didn't talk too much save for a few questions like asking why in God's name I decided to travel across the country for a job change.

I replied to him saying. "Hell if I know. I just go where my orders tend to send me."

We both got a good laugh out of it and started talking about our days in the military and how we both got to our current standing in life. Turns out we had more in common than I thought.

Dustin Martin, as he came to be known to me, dropped me off at the ranger's post just outside the town limits.

"What's your name, son?" the chief asked. His voice was raspy, kind of a mix of R. Lee Ermey and Clint Eastwood.

"Dakota Faraday, sir."

"Good. We need some new blood out here. Too many lawbreakers thinkin' they can get away with poachin' and kids thinkin' the park is their personal party space and trashcan." Mike Thomas, the chief of the rangers I would be reporting to seemed bitter but disciplined. "You'll need a truck. Luckily we heard you was comin' and got yours looked at."

When I laid my eyes on the truck assigned to me, it wasn't special. I'd seen many like it. I'd driven many like it.

"This is yours. Take good care of her and she'll serve you well. Report tomorrow for trainin' and the tour of your station."

"Yes sir." I replied, happy to oblige him seeing as he seemed like he just wanted to go the bar and drink.

I decided to drive into town to get to know the locals.

The bar known to the town as the Dusty Shoe was, according to the folks at the gas station playing checkers, the best place to go to get to know people.

Upon stepping inside, it wasn't anything I hadn't seen before.

An old bar curved around towards the bathrooms; behind it were shelves of bottles with a tap loaded with Bud Light.

The man behind the bar was fat with an ashen gray beard wearing an old plaid shirt and jeans cleaning out one of the glasses left behind by the drunks.

"Afternoon." I said, tipping my hat and walking up to the bar and sitting. "I'd like a scotch, please."

"Ah, you the new ranger?" he asked, his voice cheerful. An Uncle Buck of a character if I ever saw one.

"I am. Dakota Faraday at your service, Mister?"

"Lawrence Gibbons. You can call me Larry." He replied, setting down a shot glass and filling it with scotch. "Where you from? I don't recognize 'at accent."

"Virginia. Good old deep accent from the small towns."

"Ah, southern boy. You're a long way from home."

"Gotta follow where the orders are, Larry. From the tattoo on your arm, I gather you understand."

Larry looked at the faded naval tattoo on his arm. A smile curved its way across his face under his wiry beard. "Sure do. Good to meet a kindred spirit." He said.

We talked a bit more about our tours in the military, laughing at the silliness of the men in power that put us in the most God-forsaken places in the world. Then sat back and took all of the glory for themselves.

When Larry walked off to go take care of another patron, my eyes wondered around the bar taking in the faces of the people I would come to know in my time in Darrington.

There were the bikers with women on their laps, old war veterans with their green and tan hats on their heads talking about their distrust of the government, the old friends playing chess. Mostly normal small town bar patrons.

Then there was her. The woman in the corner sitting by herself. My eyes grew wide as a teenager who was just seeing a woman for the first time.

She wore a rather conservative suit, almost like a lawyer would wear. The pants long and black with a white silk shirt covered with a black jacket. Her hair was pulled up in a ponytail was dark with hints of purple woven throughout the otherwise raven strands.

She wore black, round lensed reading glasses with a gold chain attached to them so she could take them off and hang them around her neck if she so chose. A truly beautiful woman.

She looked up, our eyes meeting in a single moment I'm sure would be classified as meeting one's soul mate. Each of us holding the other as if by some magical chain connected us in a spell neither one of us could break.

Eventually she broke the spell, gathering the book she was reading and hastily leaving the bar out into the rainy streets. I had to shake my head against the remains of the dizziness.

"Who was that?" I asked Larry, still dazed.

"Oh, that. That's Marney Blackthorn. Best keep your distance. Strange things go on when she's around." Larry Gibbons said, leaning in close.

"What kinds of weird things?"

"Black magic kinds of weird things. I warn you true, keep your distance. I hear she's been known to cast curses on folks she don't like."

I gave a light chuckle. I wasn't superstitious in the least so warnings about curses and black magic didn't really phase me. I paid for the drinks and headed back out to the truck.

Following the visit to the bar, I headed to the apartment building I would be calling home. I finally managed to unlock the door on the third floor after being flirted with by the local blonde tenant who took a liking to me almost immediately.

"You must be new around here? Someone as good lookin' as you usually wouldn't stay outta 'at blonde bitch's bed." Mrs. Jones, my closest neighbor came out to greet me. From what I could tell, she had a lot of cats. I could smell the litter when she opened the door.

"Yes ma'am. Just arrived."

"Ranger, eh?" she said, her voice wavering and raspy from the many cigarettes I could smell she smoked, spitting out a rather large load.

"Yes ma'am."

She reached out her hand, smiling. A true change from the bitterness just moments ago. "Good to meet ya. I promise I ain't as bad as I sounded. Just gotta make sure you're one of the good ones. From what I can tell. Ya are." She turned to head back into her apartment. "Oh and stay outta 'at blonde's bed. Lord only knows what she has swimmin' round in 'er."

I only sighed, walking into the apartment and closing the door, content on enjoying a beer before heading into bed for the night.

I didn't turn in until the wee hours of the morning and the sleep wasn't restful. My mind swam with images of Marney Blackthorn, her silver eyes as they pierced deep inside of me as though she was trying to read my soul. The words Larry spoke to me buzzing around in my head with warning and then music. Soft piano music.

I shot up in a cold sweat, the breath heaving out of my lungs like it was being sucked out of me by some unseen spirit. The room was empty save for the desk in the corner with my laptop and the books I liked to read to silence my mind.

"Just a dream." I said to myself, my hands scrubbing the length of my face. My head falling heavy back on my pillow. "Just a dream." My eyes closed, falling back into sleep.

The following morning was much the same as the one before. The rain fell softly creating a soothing melody on the roof and hood of the truck. I stood drinking my morning coffee, staring out at the cardinals and squirrels going about their daily business.

Memories of the dreams ran rampant in my mind. I leaned on my forearm against the doorframe, my teeth clenched as I tried to push the uneasy feeling in my gut away so I could get dressed in my uniform and head to the training.

Breakfast was very American consisting of bacon, toast with butter, and eggs over medium and sausage. I finished it quickly, put on my uniform and began driving out to the training which would be held with the chief.

On my way I saw a car stopped on the side of the road with its caution lights flashing. I recognized Marney immediately. She stood on the outside of her car appearing distraught.

My father always taught me to stop to help a lady in need so I pulled my truck up behind her car putting on my own flashing lights to make sure anyone coming up the road would see us.

"Mornin' Ms. Blackthorn. Need some help?" I asked, cheerfully as I walked up to her car.

She didn't say anything at first, only eyeing me cautiously. "No, thank you." She said, her voice cold and guarded.

"Mind if I take a look anyway?"

Marney stepped aside gesturing her hand towards the hood of her car in a "you're welcome to it" motion.

"Pop the hood please, ma'am." I asked politely knowing how the folks in town tended to treat her.

She opened the door, making her way towards the hood. "You a mechanic?"

"Nah but my pops and I used to work on motorcycles. Every once in a while we would get vehicles of the non-two-wheeled sort but it wasn't often." I chuckled earning a smile. "Ah, looks like one of your plugs shook loose. Not a hard fix, thankfully." I said fixing the plug before closing the hood. "Try it now."

Marney got in the driver's side, starting the car. The engine roared to life, sputtering only slightly.

"Thank you, sir."

"Please, call me Dakota. Glad to oblige. Might want to get it looked at. That sputtering was a bit much." I said, tipping my hat before walking back.

"Dakota." I stopped turning to look at her brushing a strand of her beautiful hair away from her face. "Thank you for helping me."

"Not a problem, ma'am. You have a good day."

I arrived at the duty station a few minutes early despite stopping to help Ms. Marney Blackthorn with her car. The chief arrived shortly after me.

"Mornin' Faraday, ready to start?" he asked lighting a cigarette.

"Sure am."

The chief led me through the areas I was responsible for patrolling. The local girls stopping to flirt with me after he left wishing me a good shift.

Nothing peculiar really happened during the first day until around three pm. I began hearing the soft music of a piano ringing out. I looked around to see if anyone else heard anything but no one seemed to hear it.

"Hey." A woman's soft voice called me out of the trance.

"Hey. Anything I can help you with, ma'am?"

"Not really. I'm Barbie Reynolds. Your neighbor. I heard Mrs. Jones complaining about me to you but I wanted you to know the rumors aren't true. I will admit I had entertained the idea of asking you to bed with me but I don't just sleep around with anyone. Just wanted you to know that." Barbie brushed a strand of her curly blonde hair away from her face.

"I don't believe rumors, ma'am. I appreciate the offer but I'm gonna have to decline."

"I figured you would. You didn't seem the type to sleep around either. If you aren't busy later, I wouldn't mind having you for dinner."

"Thank you, ma'am but no thank you. You have a nice day. It was nice meetin' ya." I said walking off. It didn't take much to figure out what Ms. Barbie Reynolds was up to.

The sound of the piano rang through my ears for the rest of the day. I was thankful when Bo Calhoun, my replacement showed up so I could head home.

∞

The day after would be an off day for me so I chose to put on a pair of dark blue jeans, work boots and a forest green button down shirt and head out to meet some of the folks of Darrington.

I hadn't just arrived at the supermarket when my eyes landed on Marney Blackthorn with a basket full of groceries. I hesitated to go to help her but then I couldn't stop myself and made my way over to her.

"Hey, Ms. Blackthorn, need a hand?" I asked.

"Dakota, you scared me." She said, nearly dropping her bag.

"Sorry bout that. Hey, it's cold today, would you give me the honor of maybe, I dunno, buyin' you a coffee?"

Marney smiled, closing the door to her Jeep Cherokee. "Ranger Faraday are you asking me for a coffee date?" she asked, chuckling.

"Yes ma'am, I believe I am. How's about it?"

"Are you sure? You know what folks say about me around here?"

"I don't believe in rumors ma'am and I'm not superstitious at all." I said offering my arm in a gentlemanly fashion.

Marney smiled, taking it and walked with me to the local coffee shop.

We sat down, waiting for our coffee to be made. Marney looked around seeing all of the judgement filled faces and started getting antsy.

"This was a mistake. I should go." She said trying to get up and going back out to the sidewalk.

I followed her, stopping her by taking her hand. She turned around to face me, slightly shocked. "Marney, you shouldn't let what folks think about you run your life. I think you're a wonderful woman that folks around here just don't understand and that's why they make up such silly stories."

"Maybe you should be more superstitious, Dakota." She said, pulling away from me to head back across the street to her Jeep.

I couldn't make heads or tails of the woman, sighing as I left the coffees to go back to my own truck.

∞

Sleep would be filled with dreams that night, the same as the last few nights. I tossed and turned in my bed. Marney's eyes haunting the visions accompanied by piano music.

A voice as soft as silk kept saying "Come find me in the woods" over and over until once again I shot up awake in bed.

The clock on the bedside read seven-thirty am. It was time for me to get up anyway so I took a shower, got dressed, had breakfast and coffee and drove out to Squire Park just before it was time for the gates to open.

As soon as I stepped through the gates, the sound of piano music played in my mind as it had every day I'd come here. I decided to find it as soon as the park closed to the public.

I had the closing shift that night so after everyone left, I listened to the music playing in my mind, following the direction it seemed to come from well into the night.

To my dismay I found nothing so I gave up the search and headed back to my truck to head home.

∞

Each day began feeling the same. I would go on my shift during the day and try to find the one responsible for the haunting piano music at night, winding up empty handed.

My dreams would repeat themselves. Marney then the music then the silken voice of a woman calling my name to come find her in the woods.

I decided I would take one of my off days to go through the forest to try and find the source of the music.

My search took me into a rather strange part of the woods I hadn't remembered going through before. It almost seemed as though it didn't belong there. The moon shone full above signaling how long I had been searching.

I followed the path until I was faced with a large iron gate. In the middle were large ornate vines in the shapes of flowers and what appeared to be fairies. It creaked when I pushed it open, the music more clear as I made my way up to a rather old house.

It looked like a mansion built in the customary Victorian or French, I couldn't be sure. The paint was white and faded. Vines crawled like snakes up the sides. I heard what sounded like whispering voices as I made my way closer.

To my surprise the door was unlocked, the wood creaking as I pushed it open. The floor was wood with a wooden spiral staircase leading up to the second floor.

The music was clearer than I'd ever heard it. "Hello?" I called out, following the sound up the stairs into a rather large room.

A blue light radiated throughout the room through two large glass paned windows. The music was reaching its height, coming down only when I stepped in the room.

"Excuse me, were you the one playing all this time? My apologies if I intruded." I said, stepping just inside the door.

The player closed the lid over the ivory keys, rising from the bench. I could tell from the outline of her body she was a woman.

She stepped into the light shocking me to my very core. Two thick horns protruded from behind two pointed ears. Her face was flat, almost like that of a faun I'd read about in old folklore books only her hooves were larger and not cloven. She had a longer tail with a tuft of hair at the end. Her body lithe and thin.

"Welcome mortal." I recognized the sound of her voice as the one who called to me in my dreams.

"Uh. I'm, I'm sorry for intruding."

The woman chuckled, stepping forward, her movements elven and beautiful. "There is no need to be afraid. I will not harm you. You were able to hear my music so our meeting is no coincidence."

"I beg your pardon, ma'am but…what are you?"

"You could not hope to pronounce what I am in your tongue however, if you must call me something, call me Fae kind."

"Fae? As in a magical creature?"

"Indeed."

I stuttered like a fool who played table top games. "I'm Dakota…Dakota Faraday."

Another chuckle. "I know who you are, Dakota Faraday. I have watched you for a long time now."

"Watched me?"

"Yes. Tested you and found you are indeed a keeper of a pure soul and kind heart. Now, sleep. We will meet again soon."

I found my eyes getting heavy, my body draining of its strength. It wasn't long until I was asleep.

∞

I woke the next morning in my own bed with no knowledge of how I got there, thinking the whole encounter had been yet another dream.

A knock on my door drew me out of the daze. I put my jeans on and went to the door, opening it to find none other than Marney Blackthorn standing on the porch with two cups of coffee.

"Good morning. May I come in? I brought some coffee."

I shook my head against the dizziness, nodding. "Yeah, yeah. Come on in."

Marney came in, setting the coffee on the table. "Are you alright, Cody? You look as though you've seen a ghost."

"I'm fine. Just a strange dream. How did you know my nickname?"

"It was a lucky guess. With your name being Dakota, I kind of just figured. Have you had breakfast yet?"

"No, not yet. I just woke up." I said, still dazed but slowly getting a grip on reality. "Marney, why did you come here? I thought you didn't like comin' out among folks?"

"I wanted to see you. To thank you for being so kind and to apologize for how I acted at the coffee shop. I'm not used to people being kind and actually noticing me." She smiled, handing me the coffee.

I sat down across from her. Something about her felt familiar.

The way she carried herself, the way she spoke so properly. It was as though we met before even though I'd only spoken to her twice.

"So, any plans for today?" she asked.

"Not really. I usually go hiking when the weather is nice or read when it's not."

The rain fell outside in sheets. There was definitely no hiking for me.

"What do you like to read?"

"Mostly fantasy and folklore. Sometimes paranormal detective novels."

"You like fantasy and folklore? Have you heard of the Fae?" Marney asked. The tone of her voice rose a pitch.

I thought back to the dream about the woman with horns. "Um, yes. I've just become aware of them." I said, a bit nervous.

"They're said to be keepers of the forest and lovers of music. The light Fae protect the balance against the Dark Fae who seek to cause trouble. Dark Fae are said to possessive and jealous spirits, often coveting pure hearts and souls and manipulating the dark sides of man."

I sat baffled at how much Marney knew about the legendary creatures. I listened in awe.

My phone vibrating alerted me to the chief's call. "Yes sir. I'll be right out." I got up to go put some clothes on.

"What happened?" From the sound of her voice she seemed both worried and frustrated.

"There's been an attack in the park. Walter Connelly was found dead wrapped in some strange, black vines. We aren't sure what happened."

Marney got up and followed me to my truck. "Cody, let me come with you, please."

I sighed, hesitating. "Alright but you stay close, got it?"

She nodded, jumping up into the cab.

∞

When we arrived, the scene was mortifying. Walter was sprawled out on the ground, his body pierced through by vines the likes I'd never seen before. His eyes and mouth erupted with the things, slithering and snaking around like eels or serpents.

"This is horrible. Whoever did this is a sick bastard." Chief said, taking a puff off of his cigar. "Until we find out just what the hell is goin' on we have to keep the park closed. All of the campers were evacuated this mornin'. Sorry for callin' ya in on yer day off, Faraday."

"It's alright, Chief. This is what I'm here for. Do we know his last known location before he was murdered?" I asked, kneeling down next to the corpse.

"Campin' with 'is friends from what 'is ma said. When he didn't call, she got worried. Bird watcher over there found the body." Chief nodded towards an elderly man talking to another ranger, shaking and nervous.

I didn't notice Marney next to the corpse until I turned to look at her. She was kneeling down next to the corpse mumbling something. I couldn't read her lips or tell what she was doing with her hands but I did see her touch one of the vines, incinerating it.

"Blackthorn! No civilians touchin' the crime scene!" Chief yelled at her. Marney backed off, making her way towards me as if I would shield her from the Chief's wrath.

"Marney, go wait for me by the truck, okay? There's not much more we can do here."

"Cody, I don't want you on this case. I don't want you anywhere near this." Marney spoke a language I didn't understand. Everyone froze around us. "This is beyond what mortals can handle."

"Mortals? Wait, Marney are you…?"

"Yes, I'm not human, Cody. You already knew. I know you did. I wasn't going to tell you. I had to be sure when we saw the body but you can't get near this." Marney looked up at me with tears in her eyes. Her hand petting my face. "Cody, I've fallen for you. Please, stay away from this. For your safety, please." She begged, her face against my chest.

"Marney, I'm a ranger. If someone is murdered in the woods, it's my job to try and find the one responsible. I can't stay away from this."

Marney's lips met mine, soft and loving. She seemed truly worried that I could get hurt or worse. "Then be careful." She led my ear down to her mouth. "Meet me. In the woods. Tonight." Her voice was the same as the woman in my dreams. She kissed me one more time disappearing; her spell dissipating.

"Faraday, stop standin' there like an idiot. There's nothin' more ta see." Chief said.

"Chief, did you see Marney here? Just now?"

"Who?"

"Marney Blackthorn?"

"You losin' yer mind, Faraday? There's no Blackthorn round here. She's probably at her place."

Marney had erased her presence from the minds of everyone on the scene except me. The more things progressed the weirder they became.

The night following the discovery, I made my way through the woods following the sound of Marney's voice in my mind until I came to a large tree.

The woman with hooves sat on one of the large branches. The whole place seemed otherworldly, as though it was only visiting.

"Marney?" I called out to her. She looked at me, smiling.

"In the human world, that is my name but not here. Here you would not know how to say my true name. Call me Esme. Welcome Dakota Faraday."

"Okay, Esme. What is goin' on? Obviously, I'm not dreamin' so this has to be real. Why did you choose me to reveal your secret to?"

Esme dropped down onto the ground. The leaves crunching under her hooves. "Your heart and soul are pure. You are gentle and kind with care for those other than yourself. It is something rare and beautiful. No one else was able to hear the music I played except you and here you are."

"What happened to Walt Connelly? I saw you touch the vines, heard them as though they were screaming as they were incinerated." I asked, slightly shaken.

Esme walked up to me, leaning her cheek against my chest. "In time I will tell you. I have a request of you first if I may, Dakota."

"Uh, okay."

"I have become fond of you. You have gone out of your way to take care of me as Marney and now you are here for me as Esme."

I swallowed hard as her gorgeous silver eyes met my own. Her hands going to unbutton my shirt.

"Will you make love to me, Dakota?" Her lips met mine in a soft kiss, her hands pushing the shirt down to the elbows, baring my chest.

I wasn't sure what happened next or how it happened.

One moment we were kissing. The next we were on the forest floor, our bodies pressed close to each other. I made love to Esme, the feeling unlike any I'd ever experienced. It was as if her magic flowed through me. I could feel it in my heart, my muscles, my very blood seemed filled with her magic.

I remember being exhausted afterwards. Lying beside her trying to catch my breath.

"Rest now, Dakota. It is very taxing on a mortal to make love to an immortal."

The last thing I remembered was Esme kissing me before I passed out from exhaustion.

"Cody. Cody, can you hear me?" Marney's voice sounded muffled as I tried to come out of the daze of fatigue.

"Marney? Where am I?"

"My house. Do you remember anything?"

I sat up, my body sore and tired. "Barely." My hand went to my head, rubbing it against the headache. "We…oh God." I got up out of the bed only to nearly fall over again, using the wall as support.

"Yes. You need to take it easy. Your body is still recovering."

"Christ, Marney, what are you?" I said, pushing her away from me.

"I'm a light Fae. The vines you saw in the body of Walter Connelly belonged to a dark Fae. She's the reason I'm here. She's gone out of control, causing chaos. Cody, the killing won't stop with Walter. She'll keep killing and feeding until she's stopped. That's not all." She said, her voice sullen. "Cody, she'll hunt you. She'll try to take you after she realizes I've touched you. You need to leave."

"Wait, you knew? You knew she would hunt me and you still pursued me?"

"I'm sorry. I know I shouldn't have. We usually don't pursue mortals but you were so kind to me, you were so gentle and willing to go out of your way to see me, I just couldn't help but fall in love with you. That's why I'm telling you to leave. I can bind her here until I can stop her."

Anger welled up inside of me. I knew I couldn't just leave. I had nowhere to go back to. My dad and mom were both dead and my sister moved overseas.

"I can't leave, Marney. I have nowhere to go. This is my home now."

Marney wrapped her arms around me, caressing the muscles of my stomach. "Then I'll hide you." She said, taking my wrist, wrapping a silver chain resembling the vines responsible for killing Walter around my wrist. "Don't take this off. It will shield you from her but you must be careful. She can take human form as well and will recognize the chain so do everything possible to keep it hidden from her. I love you, Dakota. I won't let her have you."

Still angry, I grabbed my shirt and boots and headed to my truck.

I didn't see Marney after that and no one in town seemed to remember her. It was raining as it did almost every day since I'd been in Darrington.

What few sunny days there were I'd spend hiking. Especially on my days off.

Not today. Today I decided to go to one of my favorite places to get coffee and breakfast, hoping to get my mind off of Marney (Esme to me).

"Want your usual today, Dakota?" Winona Windsor (no relation to Windsor and Newton), the waitress asked. She was an attractive young woman with her curly red hair and plump breasts. Someone I usually wouldn't mind taking to bed with me.

"Sounds good. Thanks Winona." I replied, my heart still heavy from not having seen Esme and the fight I'd had with Marney.

"Winona, do you know anyone named Marney Blackthorn?" I had to make sure I wasn't borderline insane.

"Can't say I do. That's a strange name though, I gotta say. Friend of yours?"

"Once she was. She was more than a friend."

I waited, playing with the coffee mug in my hand patiently trying to cope with the ache in my heart. I looked at the chain Esme put around my wrist. Its soft silver design serving as a reminder of the last cruel words I'd said.

I'd gone back to Marney's house to find it empty. When I asked the townsfolk where she'd gone, no one seemed to even remember her.

When the food was brought, I was surprised to see it wasn't Winona setting the plate down but a woman I'd never seen before.

In a town as small as Darrington, it was rare for a stranger to go unnoticed for too long. Especially one as strange as this woman.

I looked around to see that no one was moving. They'd been frozen much like that day Marney went to the crime scene where Walter Connelly was found dead.

"At last, we finally meet. I have searched for you. Hello there, Dakota Faraday." The woman said, her voice seductive and deep. She was inhumanly attractive as well with her emerald green eyes and dark cherry wood hair down to her bottom.

"Do I know you?" I replied, cautious.

"Not yet but you will soon. I'm Marceline, Esme's sister. I believe you may know her? She tried so hard to hide you from me." Marceline took my hand in hers, turning it over so my palm faced up, her finger running up each of mine. "You're so handsome, I can see why she's fond of you."

An innate sense of danger filled my body the longer I spent in Marceline's presence. Her eyes almost hungry as she stared at me.

A strange feeling of cold snaked its way up my hand through my body, paralyzing me and consuming my consciousness.

"What are you…doing to me?"

"Relax handsome, let my darkness consume your mind. Soon you will belong to me. You have been Fae touched by my sister, I can see it. She was a fool to think she could conceal you from me for too long. Soon, you will be all mine. You will be mine or I will consume your heart and soul." Marceline laughed, forcing me to leave the diner with her.

"Humans are such fragile creatures, would you not agree, Dakota?" Marceline said, her cheek resting against my bare chest, her nails softly running down the muscles of my stomach up my arm to the shackles around my wrists.

I couldn't respond, the words frozen inside of my throat, helpless against the magic holding me prisoner. My wrists bound to the same tree where Esme and I made love by chains made of the same black vines.

"Yet for all of your fragility we cannot seem but to be fascinated with you. I can truly see what Esme loves in you. You're handsome with such a pure heart and soul." Marceline took my mouth with hers. The kiss dark and possessive. "Usually seducing mortals is so easy. We merely have to use our magic to influence their greed or lust to control them but you, Dakota Faraday. Your purity protects you from such influence. Truly rare and precious."

Marceline guided my face to look at her, her body pressed close to mine. "I will possess you. I will control you or I will consume you. Mind, heart, body and soul."

My mind was hazy, the free will slowly draining from me as Marceline explored my body.

"Marceline!" Esme's voice pierced through the darkness of my mind. "Release him immediately!"

Marceline turned her head from me to look at her sister. Smirking she kissed me again, her thumb running the length of my throat. "You desire this mortal, sister? Even if his life is but a wing beat of your own?"

"You still understand nothing of the value of life, sister. Release him from your spell, now!"

"No."

The events that transpired next were a blur. The two sisters battled using what looked like magic. Each attacking, counter-attacking and defending until finally Esme made her way to me.

She raised a shield around us as she forced the black shackles to release my wrists. "Dakota. Dakota please. Stay awake." Her voice sounded muffled from the darkness trying to take hold. "No, no. Dear Gaia, please no. Dakota, please. Fight her. Dakota, I can't lose you. Please fight her."

Esme placed her hand on my chest, whispering something before I felt the darkness purged from my mind. My head ached as I tried to gasp for fresh air.

Marceline hammered at Esme's shield, her voice as she screamed "No" over and over again muffled by the shield.

Esme pulled me close to her. The tears she cried landed on my cheek, warm against the chilled night. "I'm sorry, my love. I never intended for you to get involved. I tried to send you away. Forgive me."

Marceline slammed two blades of pure darkness down on Esme's shield. It sparked and cracked until eventually it shattered like glass under the pressure.

I felt Esme lay me on the ground, my eyes watching though hazed lenses as the two sisters once again began fighting.

"I should have devoured that mortal. His pure soul would have given me the strength to defeat you once and for all!" Marceline yelled, her words spat out of her mouth in jealous hatred.

"No sister, even then things would have ended the same. You have gone out of control with your power long enough. Tonight this ends. Tonight you go back to the shadows from whence you came!" Esme's voice was loud and commanding. Her eyes glowed a magnificent white as light magic expanded out from her body.

Marceline shrieked a high pitched, defeating shriek, pushed back into the shadows. The remnants of her spell driven out of my body like poison from a wound.

My strength was sapped from me. I tried to hold onto consciousness. Esme dropped to her knees beside me, pulling me back into her lap.

"Is she…gone?" I croaked, my voice still not recovered from Marceline's spell.

"For now. I'm sorry, Dakota. I should not have drawn you into this. I love you with all of my heart but I know what must be done to protect you." Esme leaned down, kissing me so deeply it was like she was saying goodbye.

"Don't. Please don't." I begged, the last of my strength gone sending me into unconsciousness.

I woke up in my apartment, my memory foggy of the night before.

The alarm on my phone rang, vibrating on the wooden table next to my bedside.

I turned it off, grabbing my uniform from the hanger, going into the bathroom to start the shower.

The drive to Squire Park seemed less relaxing than it usually was. Something seemed like it was missing.

It was sunny outside on that particular day. The hikers and campers all waved their happy hellos while their young adult daughters flirted with me, asking if I was seeing anyone.

When I told them I wasn't they would ask for my number which I politely declined.

It was like any other day but still I felt a hole in my heart. Then came the music. The soft tune of the piano playing in the distance. I tried looking for it trying to find the source. I looked around to see if anyone else could hear it, surprised no one seemed to.

Making my way over the wooden bridge, I followed the familiar sound. No matter how far I went into the woods, I never found the piano or the one playing it.

My heart was heavy and saddened for reasons unknown to me at the time.

Things never went back to normal in Darrington. I got out of that place as soon as I could, traveling back to Virginia. For ten years I lived in pain until finally the memories were set free.

I never found Esme, never saw any other like her but still I would feel the touch of her magic, I would remember the feeling of her body, hear her voice but the only way I can relive them is to write letters like the one I wrote to you.

The words I put down here are real. The world I spoke of is real.

Don't forget them. Don't forget her.

Never forget her.

Check out more cartoons like this….
www.inkygirl.com

Island of Toys

By

William Diaz

After unpacking the last of the boxes, Darren and Agatha Chambers took a well-deserved break on their leather sofa. Since moving to their new Walmer Road Victorian - style house, almost everyone seemed to be on Cloud Nine. Eight-Year old Christie was anxious to play in her new bedroom with her new friends, ten-year old Aiden was in his bedroom, glued to the iPad that his mother tried to pry him away from. Only six-year old Maggie clung to her parents, scared and unwilling to go upstairs.

"Maggie, honey, why don't you want to play in your new room?"

Maggie vigorously shook her head. "I don't want to mommy."

Darren shot a look at his wife. "We've been here three weeks now, yet she still won't sleep in her own room."

Before Darren could continue, Agatha piped up. "Maggie, why don't you want to sleep in your room?"

Maggie pouted at first, her stringy brown hair partially hiding her eyes. "Clyde wants me to follow him to the attic."

Darren's eyes narrowed. "Who's *Clyde* honey?"

"The little huntsman."

Darren couldn't recall a huntsman toy at first, but it was Agatha who remembered. "That was Aiden's toy when he was seven; do you remember how happy he was when we brought it home? The way the little arms swung his ax..."

Darren nodded. "How can I forget, he cried for days when he thought he lost it. Turned out it was buried in his closet." He turned to his youngest daughter and lovingly said. "Honey, *Clyde* is only a toy. He can't talk. If you want, mommy or I can sleep next to you tonight. Would you like that?"

Maggie, though unconvinced, nodded.

That same evening, Darren was prepping Maggie's bed sheets when he heard a faint creak up above. He craned his head to the side, and sure enough he heard it again.

"Raccoons," he muttered.

It was almost five in the morning when little Maggie found herself alone in her bed; her father awoke early to go to work. After rubbing the sleep from her eyes, her attention was drawn to her dresser. Standing in front of it was the toy huntsman from the attic. The tiny ax in the huntsman hand had an unusual gleam to it, it appeared very real. The painted eyes of the toy huntsman went from green to blood red. *Its ok child,* the toy seems to say, *Clyde can take you to a wondrous place. Just take my hand; I will protect you with my trusty ax.* Little Maggie's lips trembled; she wailed until her mother rushed in to soothe her.

Mister and Mrs. Chambers were called into Maggie's school that afternoon. Miss Potter, the First Grade teacher met with them in an empty classroom. She had with her a file folder.

"Thank you for coming and I apologize for pulling you from your jobs." Miss Potter took a deep breath; there was a tremble as she breathed out. "As you know, here at Fern Avenue Public School we encourage our little ones to tap into their creativity as much as possible," Miss Potter bit her bottom lip. "Not only do encourage them but we as teachers also monitor their progress."

"So what's the issue?" Darren Chambers asked after a brief pause.

Miss Potter opened the file folder and produced the first drawing. "Maggie is a talented little girl; she's drawn some very nice pictures. So I was a little taken back when she drew this."

Agatha looked at the drawing, goosebumps forming on her arms. She shot a glance to her husband. "That's Aiden's toy huntsman from the attic, but she drew it with red eyes instead of the green."

Darren swallowed nervously. "I'm sure that's just Maggie's imagination running wild."

"There's more." Miss Potter pulled out the second drawing. It was the same huntsman, only depicting it with an ax; beneath it was another toy, a Humpty Dumpty, its arm already severed. There were streaks of red coloured in with a crayon, where the Humpty Dumpty's arm was cut off.

Agatha gasped. "Oh my God."

Darren Chambers looked on, his face a few shades pale. "When did Maggie start drawing these disturbing pictures?"

"About two and a half weeks ago," Miss Potter responded. "Maggie told another student that 'Clyde' had been visiting her room almost every night since moving into your new home. Says that he wants her to come up to his attic and take her to a nice place. Does any of this sound familiar?"

Agatha slowly wagged her head. "No, she's never told us about this 'Clyde,'" she lied, "or told us about going anywhere with anybody."

Darren saw that the last drawing was face down. "Is that another of Maggie's drawings?"

Miss Potter looked down, instinctively placing her hands on the picture. "I was hoping I wouldn't have to show this one." She tapped her fingers on the table. "This drawing...was the one that unsettled me the most." Miss Potter flipped the paper.

Mister and Mrs. Chambers were aghast. The same huntsman was drawn, and so were Maggie's parents and siblings. It would have been a nice picture, had it not shown a smiling huntsman with a bloody ax, holding a smiling Maggie by the hand and the Chambers family, with "x's" drawn as the eyes and little frowns on their faces, chopped up into pieces.

"I know I'm being forward," Miss Potter said. "But I would suggest taking Maggie to see a specialist who deals with abnormal child behaviors."

"No," Darren said instantly, almost on the defense. "We'll talk to Maggie, tonight."

Later that evening, Darren and Agatha asked about Aiden and Christie's day as they sat at the dinner table. All but Maggie cheerfully told their tale. When Aiden and Christie cleared their dishes and rushed away to their respective bedrooms, Darren and Agatha turned their attention to their youngest daughter.

"Maggie, honey, Miss Potter showed us some your drawings," Agatha reached out to touch her daughter's little hand. "Maggie, your teacher thinks you can draw nice pictures, but what she's shown us today is...is there anything you'd like to tell us?"

Maggie folded her arms and pouted. "Clyde keeps coming to my room. He wants to take me somewhere." In a lower voice she murmured. "I don't want to go."

Mr. Chambers slid closer to little Maggie, putting her arm around the little girl. "Honey, I find that hard to believe. That toy used to belong to your brother, if you want, I can hide it for you."

"Ok," Maggie muttered in a small voice.

Right after tucking the kids in bed, Darren Chambers climbed the steps up to the attic. From the first day moving into the new house Darren never liked the attic. Though not a religious man, Darren had cold chills every time he climbed up to the almost one hundred year old attic.

Darren reached the top of the attic stairs. He almost turned around but vigorously shook his head. "This is ridiculous," he muttered. "I'm a grown adult."

The attic's flooring creaked with Darren's weight. He scanned about him, noticing taped up boxes and an antique cabinet in a dark corner that had been left behind by the previous owner. A flash of forest green caught Darren's eye; Aiden's toy huntsman. The small axe held firm in its hands. It sported a mini green tunic, brown leggings and tiny black boots. The little huntsman was propped up on top of one of the boxes.

"Aiden...I'm going to have a talk with the little devil for scaring his sister." Darren turned to leave when a thought entered his mind.

It was me.

He froze, icy cold spider legs crawled down his spine. He glanced back at the toy huntsman still propped on the box. Darren did not want to admit it, but he felt as though the toy was staring right at him, as though it wanted to communicate with him. Darren hurried to the stairs; he did not look back to see the toy huntsman waddling to where Darren stood moments ago, watching intently but staying out of sight.

Two days later Darren's real estate agent, Ricardo Sandoval was sitting in the Chamber's living room.

"Thank you for coming on such short notice, Ricardo," Darren said as he and Agatha shook hands with the agent.

"Not a problem Darren," Ricardo said with a light trace of a Salvadoran accent. "You know, I have to admit, your urgent request to know the history of your home over a week ago caught me off guard." Ricardo slid the folder across to Agatha, thick with loose leaf papers and newspaper clippings. "I apologize if it took me this long to gather the information you requested, but better late than never."

After the children had gone to sleep, Darren and Agatha pulled up in their study and began poring over the folder. Darren had not told his wife about his uncomfortable experience in the attic.

They flipped through the mundane paperwork of deeds, titles and agreements. The one hundred year history of residents of the Walmer house was found at the bottom of the pile. Agatha pulled out a newspaper clip, dated back to August, nineteen-eighty two that caught her eye. Her eyes went wide. "*Jesus.*"

Darren snatched the article and began to read it out loud."...police were called to the Baldwin residence just after four this morning after neighbours witnessed a screaming woman thrown from the top floor of the house. Police discovered the bodies of all four Baldwin children: eleven year old twins Darcy and Danielle, nine year old Joseph and six year old Kenneth with multiple stab wounds to the torso. All four children were found tied up in the family attic. Forty-nine year old Clyde Baldwin was found dead with a self-inflicted slash wound to the throat. Sources say the Baldwin family seemed normal the night before the killings; greeting neighbors..."

"Darren, you need to see this," Agatha said as she handed her husband another newspaper clip of the Baldwin murder-suicide. Darren looked at the photos taken of the attic, and paled. The pictures showed the attic walls scrawled with markings of "666" and upside down pentagrams and crosses. On the floor of the attic was another image more terrifying than the first; it was the image of a four eyed demon sitting on a throne with arms spread open.

"Holy shit," he cursed. "My stomach is in knots right now. You think Maggie calling the toy huntsman 'Clyde' is any coincidence?"

"It seems like it..." Agatha's hand absently brushed on the yellow stained file folder. She gasped when she read the contents. "This house was purchased by the wealthy Barnabas family one hundred years ago. It was passed down from generation to generation, each one more evil than the last." Agatha found another sheet of paper. "According to this last known Barnabas family member, his kin, we're engaged in animal sacrifices, orgies, Satanic rituals, the last of his people even went as far as...*oh my God*, ritual murder."

Darren finished reading the rest of the report. "The victims were cleverly chosen. They were people of lower class; prostitutes, winos, the mentally unstable and in some cases, disowned relatives and children of the wealthy. Then the house went up for auction when the surviving Barnabas members vanished without a trace. There's even more reports of strange occurrences: sounds from the attic at three in the morning, screaming throughout the house, shadows of evil entities and so on." Darren paused before wiping his brow. "We should have suspected something was up when we bought the house at a low price..."

Clyde the huntsman stood at the vent, listening. His eyes swirled a bright red when he heard the man named Darren, Maggie's father says, "*We need to sell.*"

"No," Clyde said, his painted smiley faces betraying nothing. "With my trusty ax this family will never leave from here." Clyde cackled a wicked laugh.

"I want to sleep in your bed mommy," Maggie pleaded.

"Maggie, honey, you're a big girl...you need to sleep in your own bed like your siblings."

The little girl shook her head. Darren and Agatha looked at each other, sighing.

"Fine," her father said, "but when mommy and I say lights out, it's lights out."

It was three o'clock in the morning when Maggie was awoken by a shuffling noise along the floor. Clyde the toy huntsman propped himself on the nightstand, staring at her with luminous red eyes. *Sssh, do not be afraid child; I am here to take you to a special place.*

Maggie remained frozen in place, lips trembling, but unable to produce a sound.

Good, very good my little Maggie. But first...

Clyde hopped onto the bed into Maggie's lap. His luminous red eyes began swirl, hypnotizing the little girl. *You are my child.* The toy huntsman said with a hush, *you belong to me now.*

Any fear that Maggie felt, had evaporated like a morning fog in the sunlight. Her face was one of tranquillity as she slid off the bed and followed Clyde to the attic. *That's right Maggie, go up and wait for me.*

The toy huntsman hopped up onto the bed again next to Agatha Chambers. He raised his little axe, a sliver of moonlight gleaming off the deadly blade.

Beside Agatha, Darren began to stir. His eyes opened; he stiffened, then sat up in an instant. Agatha's throat was cut open. He looked down to see that his bed sheets were covered in his wife's blood. Darren's own blood ran cold when he saw the empty space next to his deceased Agatha.

"Maggie," he whispered. Even before he saw the trail of blood on the hardwood floors, Darren knew where Maggie went.

The flight up the attic stairs was the longest Darren had ever felt. He'd stumbled a few times, cursing himself for nearly waking his other two children. He hesitated when he reached the attic door. *This has to be a nightmare.*

The door opened with a loud creak. Darren inched his way across the attic floor. Once his eyes adjusted to the dark, Darren saw two shadows shuffling into the cabinet. Two small shadows the same height as his older children.

Then it hit him. "Aiden! Christie! What are--?"

Darren felt a stinging sensation in his Achilles heels. He fell to his knees, fighting hard to not scream, and then dropped to his side when Darren was struck again. He looked up, with eyes as wide as saucers and too injured to defend himself, to see Clyde the toy huntsman looming over him with his bloody ax.

Although the mouth made no movements, Darren Chambers heard the words resonate in his mind from Clyde as he lifted his little but deadly ax. "With my trusty ax, you will never leave!" Over and over again the blade rose and fell until Darren was no longer moving. Satisfied with his work, Clyde scrambled back into the cabinet. "I will return for you," he said.

Maggie was in her trance the whole time, including when her siblings marched into the cabinet.

The toy huntsman returned. "Take my hand little Maggie," Clyde said. Maggie clutched the toy huntsman's hand and was led into the cabinet.

An island appeared before them. Toys could be seen as far as the eye can see. Toys in the sand, toys hung in the trees, broken toys, discarded toys...toys everywhere.

At first Maggie was elated, until she saw a pair of boy and girl toys with brown hair, hung from a branch...

"Is that my brother and sister?" Maggie asked.

"Why yes," Clyde responded.

Maggie shrieked. "They're toys...you've turned them into toys!" Maggie tried to move. "What is happening to me Clyde?"

"Precious Maggie," there was a deep, guttural sound in Clyde's voice. "As I told you, I took you to a nice place, and here you are." Clyde picked up Maggie, now a doll, grabbed a line from a nearby spool and tied her to a tree next to Aiden and Christie. He cackled his horrendous laugh as he finished with the knot.

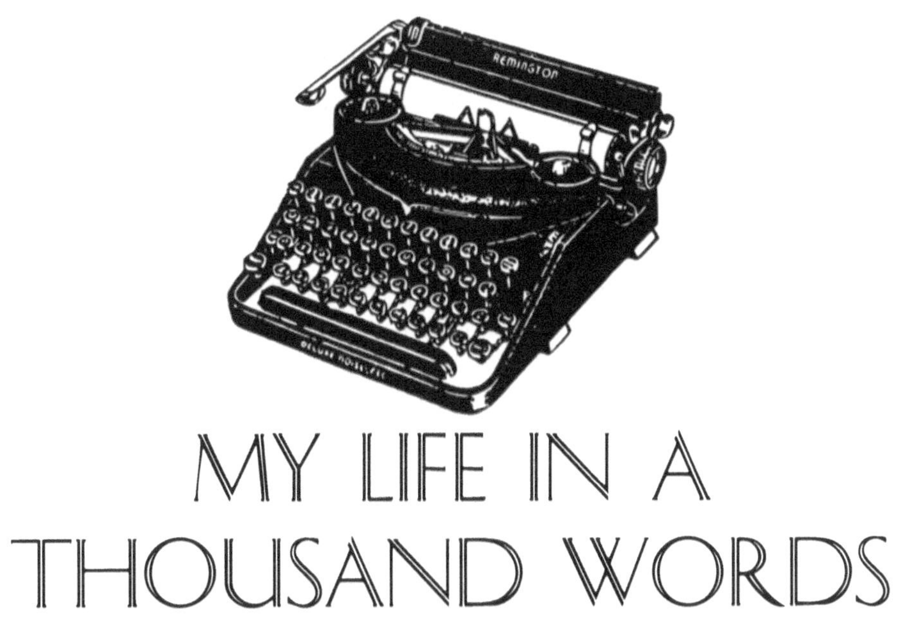

MY LIFE IN A THOUSAND WORDS

By

Marcus Blake

The man stood outside the bar waiting, waiting for the man who ruined his life. He was beat down; tired, and suffering from the worst hangover in his life, but there he stood waiting. All he could think about was the man who destroyed everything he had and of course that's when revenge seemed possible. He had a true enemy in the man he waited for and his enemy had struck a deadly blow. The bar he was in front of was called Jake's downtown bar and it was the regular hangout for the man he waited for. Vincent was his name, the man who ruined his life, and he'd done it in a thousand words.

The man waited 20 minutes while patrons from the bar gave him dirty looks as they walked in and out; they gave him the same disdained looks as they would a junkie or homeless person. Finally the moment arrived, Vincent showed up for his afternoon drink, it was his daily break from the grind of deadlines and endless typing that never seemed to make sense. He said "hi" to the usual crowd that stood outside the bar and he knew like his own family. As he was shaking a friend's hand the man who had been waiting pulled a gun from his jacket and grabbed Vincent pushing him down to the ground. He waved the gun in his face. Vincent had a look of terror on his face, not knowing what to make of the situation. It wasn't the first time he'd had a gun waved at him, but other times he had been too drunk or stoned to care. They were his Hunter Thompson moments and now he was looking for one again, but this time he came up short as he was being forced to face his demons.

The man with gun waved the gun at the crowd outside the bar waving them back so he would not be crowded. He picked Vincent up and led him into the bar and then told everybody to get out or he would start killing people. A few moments later the bar was empty except the man with the gun, Vincent, and the bartender. The man with the gun after putting Vincent in one of the booths by force finally asked him.

"Why did you do it, man?"

"Do what sir?" Vincent asked him, trying to be polite at the same time as not to upset the man with the gun.

"You know what you did, you ruined my life."

"How did I ruin your life? I don't even know you and I think you have to know somebody to ruin their life."

"Don't be fucking smart with me."

"I'm not trying to be sir, but I honestly don't know what you're talking about."

"It's what you wrote man."

"I write lots of things, can you be more specific?"

The man with the gun walked over and hit Vincent in the head with his gun. Then he replied "I'm the cop you wrote about. The article said I hate niggers."

"I know who you are now and I never said that in my column."

"But you were thinking it and you implied it you fucking bastard. Do you know how much shit I have to put up with now, I can't even work thanks to you."

Vincent just stared at the man with a fun, he wasn't even afraid anymore, he was guilty and then in a moment's flash his guilt turned to anger. He replied to the man. "I don't write anything that isn't true."

When he said that, man with the gun got even angrier. He pulled the cocking hammer back on the gun as if he was about to finally shoot, but then he stopped. He said to Vincent "Fuck you, you still don't know what you're talking about. You can only right the truth if you really know what happened. You weren't there, how would you know?"

"There were witnesses to what happened, I have their accounts."

"I was alone when it happened, people will say what they have to just to protect themselves."

Vincent sighed for a moment. He adjusted himself in the booth to sit more comfortably. Then looked directly at the man with the gun and said. "Be honest with yourself, you could have done things differently, you could have done things better. You made a mistake and I called you on it."

"We all make mistakes, but in the heat of the moment when you're staring down the barrel of gun that's when we're our true selves and that's when we let the fear dictate our actions. What do you do when you're faced with that kind of fear?"

"I don't know."

"Exactly, you don't."

"But could you have done something differently?"

"Maybe, but I didn't. Should I be punished all my life for it? Does my life have to end with that one single moment?"

"You killed somebody; you can't just walk away from that. You should have to live with it."

The man with the gun started to drop the gun as he stared at Vincent at the utter shock at what he said. He couldn't believe the arrogance and self-righteous attitude of Vincent. He lifted the gun again pointing it at Vincent to make him cower in fear then he stopped. He said to Vincent. "You know, you're right. So you'll have to live with the death of your friend." Then the man with the gun pointed it at the bartender and shot him three times. After he did Vincent screamed at him in anger to stop because it wasn't too late. The gun crazed man looked at Vincent and said his last words. "I hope somebody will write about this, it should only take a thousand words." He shot himself in the head after that. Vincent ran behind the bar to help his friend Jim – it was too late, he was already dead.

***** Part of the 1,000 Word Short Story Project*****
Can you write a short story in exactly 1,000 Words?

Will Write For Chocolate

by Debbie Ridpath Ohi

WillWriteForChocolate.com

Twitter: @inkyelbows

Check out more cartoons like this....
www.willwriteforchocolate.com

POETRY

Poetry is when an emotion has found its thought and the thought has found words.

~ *Robert Frost*

Words

Words sweep softly out the mouths of doves,
And nestled neatly, on some park bench or cushioned seat
form a blanket of trust.

Quick light and fleeting, whispers form, and dance around
the ears of lovers in a car, holding hands as they talk.
Alone in their world, Alone in plain view.

Words creating private rooms and shelters against storms
of stress,
An empty gaze, cold and devoid, brightens at a word, a
song, a story.

Angst and fears are sent sailing away on the tides of a
solitary sentiment,
Momentary, motionless, more than a lifetime, met gazes
mold lips against each other.

And in the beat of a heart and breath taken, echo out the
words "I love you,"
Words upon words, begin lifetimes of memories, opened
hearts, open arms, open lives.

Words, that give, that create, that build,
Words, that heal, that protect, that save.

But words are imperfect, they may decay, may hurt,

may scar,
Words may tear, rip and claw.

Torrents and tirades, red tinged regret, stinging at the soul
of a dove,
With wings like Icarus two beings fall, weightless, heavy,
and cold.

Words trap, tempt, and take,
Like chains on the ankles of a man, who crawling against
fate.

Pulling himself up and banging at the door of a girl
Breathlessly whispers, "I won't give up."

Words are the response, and somewhere, among the angst,
among the stress and fear,
A dove whispers back, "Neither will I."

~ Brooks Ordich

Enigmatic

She was but a glimpse,
A single feather falls,
From heavenly skies.
My angel on my shoulder,
A million things I'd say,
About this life I've lived.

Come sit by me by my feet,
And listen to my words.
I'm an enigmatic soul.
No grass grows beneath me.

~ Robin McNamara

This Kind

Life stands still when your name is spoken.
Though the ocean runs deep to a dark bottomless end,
Yet still my love surpasses its profundity in weight.
This "kind" has to come with a price
A price that sure cannot be compensated with trivial earthly
exchange
This "kind" provokes rage and humbleness
Trials and triumphs
Insecurities and assurance
It cannot be bound by the mountains and valleys of everyday
circumstance
And will not bow down to the ordinary
Oh, the wretch it has made me at times
Yet the fiery ocean tides have washed away the impurities of
 Mistrust and conflict.
And refined me into a more polished and elated soul.
The journey has been long but worth it all
Joy has taken over the happy which needed something to
"happen" to exist
The joy is here no matter how the season may transform
Joy can travel to the pits of hell to retrieve my love
And redeem its weight without time passing by
It can reach down to the inner most parts of the earth,
Where my human eyes are constraint
And convey the assurance of my commitment to my love
In places where there
Is doubt.
This "kind" is worth it.........

~ Kayvonna K. Stigall

Beware of Dogs

I think
They speak before they think
Like Dogs they'd lick their pokes.

I also think
They're con men
With words they'd romance you
And make love to you
Until they've impregnated you
With promises.

They say good morning
But they meant give me your money, they claim'
they're servants
But they're Oga and Madame.

Like vultures
They feast and prey on their pawns
Rather than plough the land
They plundered the land
Until the land is recession'

Beware of legis-looters
Beware of execu-thieves
Beware of judi-sharing
Beware of civil-devils
Beware of dogs.

~ Emeyazia Chukwudi

CAN YOU TELL US, HOW ARE YOU GOING TO DEAL WITH THE ENVIRONMENTAL ISSUES?
HAHAHAA..... I SAID THAT, I WANT QUESTIONS ABOUT IMPORTANT ISSUES.... COME ON WHAT IS ENVIRONMENT......
POLITICIANS

Death

What is life without it?
Would there be life,
Without its opposite?
The tick of the clock,
The walls caving in.
Could there be good,
Without any sin?
Light wouldn't be nothing
Without its darkest shadow.
Will the depths of darkness,
Reveal a true glow?

My sweet surrender
Is not a concern.
I do know one thing.
We all get our turn.

~ Danette Nichole Torgeson

Pins

I'm holding on to the now
In this room, that I know so well
Random sketches of anxious youth
Girls and guys
And wide, nervous eyes
Fall from the wall
Grasped merely by pins

Dozens of pins forced through
Vision boards
French awards
Old and new friends
Past and present trends
The person I was then
The person I am now

In five months' time
I will be in a new room
Tacking new sketches
Photos and awards
But the things
That will remain
The things that hold me together
The pins.

~ Savanna Rose

Spiraling Out

I met you like the sun meets the moon,
For a while, I wasn't meant to stay
It seems time passed by too soon
And both of us knew I had to go away.

Once you said, it's about what could've been
Now it's about what didn't happen,
Taking the universes time in vain
I hope to see you sometime again

~ Juliana Rodriguez

Forevermore

Gentle heart you have
Not like mine, softer
The way you touch
The way you talk
The way your eyes dance of happiness
Your smile…endless
Make my heart sing
I've created you once, carried you, fed you
Sheltered you, taught you what I know
The reality is though
You've given me more, taught me more
Created more, molded me more
Growing close to you
Is love forevermore

~ Martine Phillips

Solstice

If I go to March,
And I met you April,
Would you introduce me,
To May?
And promise to take me,
To June?
Will you be my Summer,
As I reach the Autumn,
Of my life.
Our time together so short,
Like Winter's Solstice.

~ Robin McNamara

Check out more cartoons like this….
www.leftycartoons.com

Divinity

Away from the world of duality,
There exists another land,
Which lies undiscovered by living being,
Deep within lies divinity,
Bliss and ecstasy,
Covered by layers of dust,
Cleansing of the same,
Blooms everyone like a flower,
There is so much treasure,
So many jewels,
Which we hunt outside,
When the doors within open there is
So much peace and solace,
Which can never be found in the outer world

~ Vandana Bhatnagar

The Throne

1

Saved by Grace, by Grace ye sit
In Divine respite from toil and sweat
For He giveth thus, each one thine own
Thy allotted time upon The Throne.

2

As cheeks ensconced on porcelain freeze,
From feotid aeries Judgement's squeezed.
Tween twats or testes, taints proceed
To mete out sentences decreed.

3

Thy amber grog with loo cakes brown,
Force-fed each time thy gavel sounds
To knaves and blackguards, tarts and twits,
Fish-shrews, fops, and cutpursettes.

4

With reverence wipe, then flush in prayer;
Of tank-less chamber pots beware.
And now and then take pause, perchance,
To reflect upon Thy recompense:

5

In Defecation, so in Death.
Thy noble titles are bereft.
We all are Musketeers bare bummed.
One Throne for all and all for One!

@ by - The Right Honorable Sir Richard Hedd,
1st Viscount Porte-San, 67 Bow St., London,
this 14th day of February, in the year of Our Lord, 1729

HAIKU
Themes

January 2019 Theme

"The New Year"

Little fire, dwindle.
Swelling seas, recede. For now.
Next will be your year.

~ Ryan Miller

A toast to the new.
One more year of this great life
Between me and you.

~ Marcus Blake

Sunlight of the North
Sweeps calming fingers across
East to West again.

~ Ryan Miller

A New Year is here.
Forgot about New Year's Eve,
I'm still hungover

~ Marcus Blake

Just one favor for
Three hundred sixty five days:
Please shut the fuck up.

~ Ryan Miller

Check out more cartoons like this….
www.leftycartoons.com

Finally, Linda was able to identify the
source of her writer's block.

©2011 Debbie Ridpath Ohi & S.G. Redling · Inkygirl.com · Twitter: @inkyelbows.

Check out more cartoons like this....
www.inkygirl.com

Check out more cartoons like this….
www.leftycartoons.com

Articles *and* Editorials

Life Lessons from Grief

By Allison Costa

It's hard to believe that it has been almost four years since my father passed away. Reflecting back, those horribly freezing cold weeks seem as if they were a dream, and yet are as vivid as if they were only a moment ago. I also realize that even though what everyone says is true, the first year after a loved one dies is always the hardest, it doesn't exactly get easier. It just gets becomes more of a reality, instead of constantly feeling like you are waking from a nightmare, you just become more accustomed to the emptiness. When my father passed away, it happened during the coldest ice storm that Texas had seen in about seven years. It was depressing, and yet fitting that the earth should mourn my father's life the same way that I was. To add to the grief and shock we were feeling, my own little family of 8 was experiencing a lot of bad luck. My older children had picked up lice while I watched my friend's kid, our washing machine had broken, and all my kids got food poisoning from a cub scout banquet we attended the day after my dad passed. Three days after his passing was also my wedding anniversary. My husband and I both cried, saying that one day it would make a great story that on our 11th anniversary we were cleaning up puke, combing out lice, and trying to change our spring break plans to accommodate a funeral.

One day. My sweet middle daughter turned six on the day of my father's viewing. We went to the beach that morning and had cake and presents later that night, after I had spent hours at my father's viewing greeting old friends and sobbing my guts out. I know it sounds odd, but the juggling of the normal with the surreal is all that helped me survive those difficult days. Sometimes I think it is the normalcy of life with small children that has helped me cope these last few years as well.

My father's death happened so quickly and unexpectedly, that it truly took all of the first year he was gone to even process. The pain and the loss still feels so fresh and so raw, that I find myself sobbing from the smallest memory. Out of nowhere it can all come rushing back. That's because there is not a time limit on grief. Even when our lives keep going, we grieve for the rest of our lives. Even when we experience joy and happiness, the grief becomes a part of our human experience. Our joys become deeper because we have experienced such a loss. At times my heart still doesn't quite accept that he is gone. Four months after he passed, I would still text his phone with funny comments and little quips that were part of our everyday banter. I keep our last text messages saved on my phone as a treasure, and could kick myself for all of the texts and voicemails that I erased. Ironically, on my first birthday a couple of months after he passed, I found an old voicemail of him calling and singing happy birthday to one of my sons. It was so good to hear his voice, but I was racked with sobs for a while. Death is like that. It is a thief that sneaks up on you again and again--even after what you love has been stolen you can still feel the loss so intently months and years later.

Six months before my dad died, I gave birth to my sixth child. My water broke at 9:30pm on my kids second day of school. I had planned to drive myself to the birthing center and have my husband meet me there, but my father insisted upon taking me. I could tell how nervous he was as we drove in semi-silence. I remember assuring him that we would make it with plenty of time. He told me he wasn't worried, even though I could see his knuckles white with fear on the steering wheel.

After he passed this memory became so special. The significance was not lost on me. My father was driving his sixth child, to deliver her sixth child. How poignant it would all seem just 6 months later once he was gone. I know that my baby girl will not remember her Papa at all. Sadly, most of my children will not remember him well because they were all so young. But I am so incredibly grateful that he got to meet all of them. We can learn a lot from death, and if the weeks during his rapid illness and decline in the hospital taught me anything it is gratitude. Gratitude for how much we have been given; grateful for memories to hold on too. In my fathers' death somehow I also found the joy of life. I found the importance of knowing that each moment—for good or bad—could be someone's last impression of you or yours of them. So take the pictures. Give them hugs. Realize that "this too shall pass". Know that the child who will not sleep in their own bed, potty train or give up their "binki," eventually will, and they will always remember the love you showed them. Put forth the extra effort even when it isn't convenient. Say what you need to say. Be better. Be kinder. Forgive often. Let go. Smile. Laugh. Cry. Experience moments to their very fullest. Give service often, with love and an open heart. Remember that each human being you encounter is full of their own pain, losses, and complexities and respect that.

Most importantly, know that your life is enough just the way it is. Don't waste any more time wishing away the monotony of your days, or the simplicity of your relationships. Those moments will be the ones you cherish the most when all is said and done.

©2010 Debbie Ridpath Ohi. URL: Inkygirl.com. Twitter: @inkyelbows.

Check out more cartoons like this....
www.inkygirl.com

IS VIRTUAL WORLD IMPERILING THE REAL WORLD?

By

Amay Saxena

Social media aficionados are taking the process of problem-solving to the next level. Before the Era of Social Networking, there was a traditional method for solving – that is – by thinking. Now, more often than not, people post their problems on Facebook and other social networking sites to find solutions, making it public and asking for views from others. The difference between the social and private life is decreasing, and people are realizing that nothing is working out for them. They aren't able to find a place for them in the virtual world, and in that process, they are losing themselves in the real world.

A jillion of popular Facebook pages post images of a public figure, or a politician, followed by a joke, and within an hour, the post receives about 10,000+ likes and 5,000+ comments. It is safe to assume Social Networking sites as platforms, for the commoners, to share their opinions on. But, it does have a huge drawback. And, it is – virality of misinformation. When a politically incorrect news story breaks online, someone usually makes a funny meme out of it, and the post goes viral. As the post goes viral, people go gaga like chimpanzees. People are drawn to comment on such matters. People can't avoid political or national issues and will give their opinion wherever the need arises. However, their opinion on the matter is only restricted to the comment section on social media. This generation is leveraging the power of the internet to earn money, share knowledge, and assist others, but they also stir unwanted hype, mostly for popularity. People often declare that, regardless of internet booming around the globe, social media sites must not be taken gravely, but Social media pages have succeeded in grabbing people's attention to trivial issues and devaluing the matters of concern. Which, indeed, require everybody's attention!

Recently, Formula One's World Champion Lewis Hamilton, while questioning Formula One's policy of organizing races in some new countries, stated: *I have been to India before to a race which was strange because India was such a poor place, yet we had this massive, beautiful Grand Prix track in the middle of nowhere.*

This derogatory remark (as found by the netizens) drew a lot of hate and insulting comments, through the popular site, Twitter, where almost everyday people, from all around the world, troll each other. However, after a day's time, Lewis Hamilton clarified his real aim behind making such a comment, which was quite logical and can better be understood with the help of the following image:

Please read 

Hey everyone. I noticed some people are upset with my comment on India. First off, India is one of the most beautiful places in the world. The culture there is incredible. I have visited and always had an amazing time however whilst it's the fasted growing economy it also has a lot of poverty. My reference was that a Grand Prix there felt strange to drive past homeless people and then arrive in an huge arena where money was not an issue.

They spent hundreds of millions on that track that is now never used. That money could have been spent on schools or homes for those in need. When we did have the race, nobody came because it was too expensive most likely or no interest. However I have met some amazing Indian fans.

This shows we are so drawn to baseless issues that we turn a blind eye to major ones. What has happened to India? Why are funny jokes, memes, and videos born out of serious issues? Why are we trying put our emotions in form of emojis? Well, there is an answer, but not so sure if it's correct.

It is a transition period for all of us. Technological advancements have benefited us. People are content with posting controversial comments, sharing useless memes, and writing jokes of FB walls. But we need to do get out of the virtual world and start living in reality. We need to work towards developing a better world. We should be sensitive while discussing issues like rape directly, as opposed to making comments on social media. Rather than finding solutions to our problems online, we must deal with them ourselves. We need to draw a line between our social and private lives. That's how we will be able to address the right issues in the correct manner.

Here, I'd like to end the article by asking a pertinent question: Talking about change and blaming others is cool in the virtual zone, but what use would it be if we cease to exist physically?

Check out more cartoons like this….
www.leftycartoons.com

Army vs. Navy

How a Football Game Teaches Us One of the Greatest Lessons in Life

By

Marcus Blake

It's hard to imagine that a simple football game could give us the greatest lesson about civility and respect. But then again, who would've thought that we would need such a lesson in this day and age. However, here we are... the most divisive time in American society since the Civil War. The idea of civility seems like an afterthought. Once Upon a Time we had such a thing. We could respect each other despite our different beliefs. We didn't care who one another voted for. Our politics or religion didn't matter. We could just exist within the same community and be friends or neighbors despite our differences. But not today.

Our hatred boils over when it comes to people who disagree with us. We have found hate within ourselves that we didn't even know existed. The friendships that we once had are gone because we care more about the things that divide us than the things we have in common. We are blinded from the belief that we are absolutely right and those who disagree with us are absolutely wrong. We have become what Winston Churchill defined as "fanatics, "people who cannot change their mind and refuse to change the subject." And now we live in a time when respect and civility are like mythical words that sound good and wishing they were true, but are just a myth.

However, there is one football game every year that shows us what respect and civility truly are. It is my favorite college football game every year, the one game that I look forward to more than any other. It is the Army / Navy game, a hard-fought football game, sometimes in the rain or the mud or even the snow between the two most revered branches of the US Military. On the outside it seems just like a simple football game between two Military Academy's, but it is a lot more than that. It is what some call a Game of Honor, a name that doesn't get used with any other football game. And more than anything, it is a game between men who have the greatest respect for one another because no matter who wins or loses, they are on the same side. The men who play this game are soldiers, where respect and civility are part of their core fiber.

For those who have ever served, they understand this. Respect and civility are ingrained in them from the first day they enter the service. And they find that common ground that we all should walk upon in order to exist in a civil society. Most of the time that common ground is just knowing that they have spilled the same blood, gone through the same shit when it comes to training, and side by side, waded through what soldiers affectionately called the "suck." Yes, this is more than just a football game. It is the perfect life lesson on how to get along and coexist with one another. Because when the battle is done and no matter who has won the game these soldiers are still one and the same. The same folks who walk that hallowed common ground and learn to exist beyond their differences.

For me, the game is very important. It is a time when fellow veterans can get together and not only enjoy a great football game, but enjoy each other's company on common ground. No matter what our politics are or our religion. No matter what our differences may be, we can get together, harass each other, tell jokes, talk trash one another, but still shake each other's hand as brothers and sister, and more importantly, friends when the game is done. We remember all things that we have in common and that they are stronger than that which divides us. We are not defined by our differences and we celebrate the common thread that brings us together. Some might say it's only for a football game, but it is an idea that applies to all spectrums of life. It is a lesson that should be practiced more. Many of us grew up playing sports. One of the earliest lessons that we learned was about sportsmanship... that it's more important how you play the game than whether you win or lose. Sure, it sounds like something we tell little kids so that they don't whine when they lose, but many of us forget that it's those lessons we should carry with us every day.. As adults, it's easy to forget, especially when it's easier to be angry over that which we dislike.

Yes, it may just be a football game to some, but the lessons that we can learn from such a simple game can make us better people. They can make a more civilized society and wouldn't that be something in this day and age. So when I hear some jackass on the news spewing propaganda or read hate fueled messages on social media, I think about the Army / Navy Game and wouldn't it just be nice if we could all get together, enjoy each other's company, and forget the things that divide us even its just for a football game. Could we be like the players at the end of the game who walk across the field shake each other's hand and exemplify the ultimate level of respect for one another? I dream that we can as a society. I dream that civility and respect aren't just meaningless words. And maybe...just maybe everyone will see that what may seem like a simple football game will teach us one of the greatest lessons in life. Civility and respect are the engines that keep the world running so that civilization doesn't crumble into oblivion. And perhaps that's why the Army / Navy Game is the most important college football game every year. From the lessons it can teach us to the camaraderie among fans of the game, it has the greatest impact on our life… far beyond any championship game.

Check out more cartoons like this….
www.lukesurl.com

But she never said "NO"

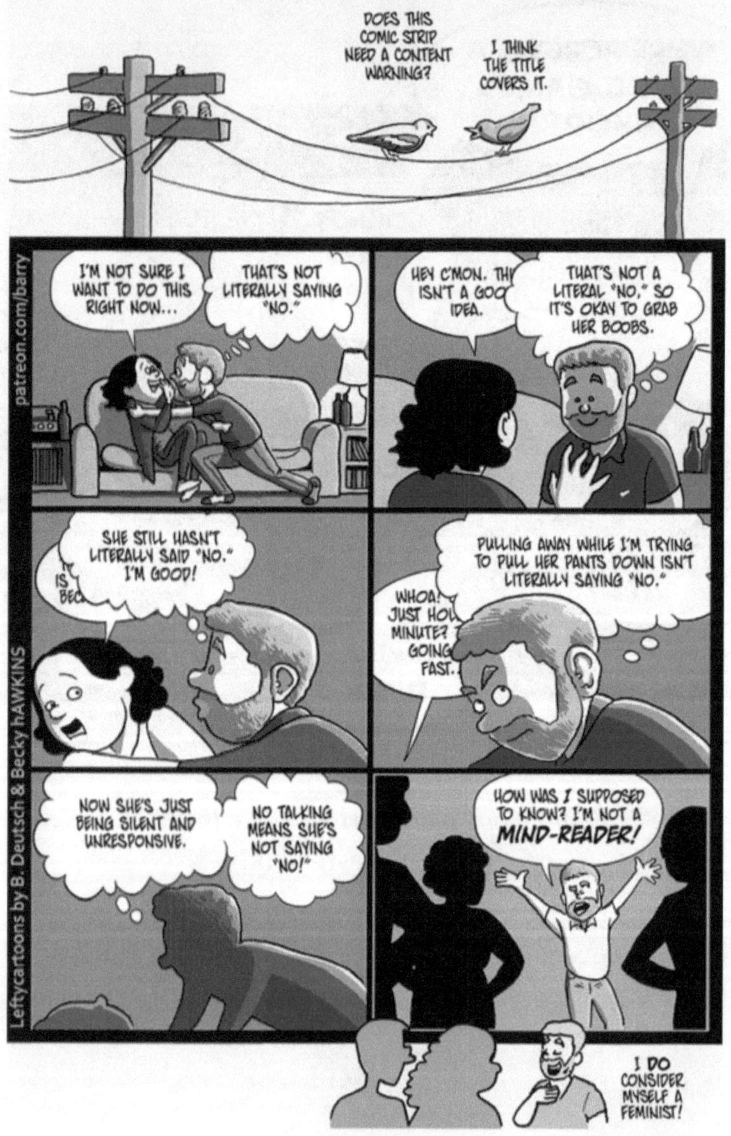

A MIXED BAG *Of* FACT and FICTION

The Disenfranchisement of White America

By Bob Jensen

For years now, a small group of Americans have claimed that there has been a disenfranchisement of White America. Most people assumed that it was just rhetoric from a small fringe group in American society. Some folks still longing for the days of the 1950's and segregation. But in recent years, this group has grown especially since the 2016 Presidential Election. It is not only white supremacist or white nationalist as some call themselves, but regular far right conservative Americans calling for a simpler time when America was great. They call it a time when there were plenty of jobs, lower taxes, and America had values.

Most of the time claims like this could be ignored as outlandish, out of touch, and hateful rhetoric that sounded more like a conspiracy theory from the X-Files. These days it seems that they are becoming more real. It was finally time for me to investigate. It was time to see the cause of these claims and get to the heart of the matter. So I went on the road and interviewed the working-class conservative Americans who were making these claims. I wanted to look at the history of where these arguments really came from. It's true that 99% of this group supported Donald Trump in the

2016 presidential election, but I feel that this is just a coincidence. It has no bearing on this article whatsoever.

The earliest claims for the disenfranchised of White America can go all the way back to the civil rights movement in the 1960s. However, it was really the start of affirmative action policies of the federal government that the claims became more widely used by far-right conservative Americans. But up until 2 years ago, it was just rhetoric that you found on the internet or social media. Except for a few lawsuits when it came to admission standards, no serious litigation has ever been brought on behalf of White America. The issue became more serious with the violent protests in Chancellorsville, Virginia when a white supremacist ran his car into a crowd of protesters linked to the Black Lives Matter movement. For the first time, the United States Justice Department took the issue seriously and under President Donald Trump's Administration has created initiatives to curtail the problem of the disenfranchisement of White America.

I recently sat down with a senior spokesperson for the US Justice Department who will remain nameless as this issue is sure to be controversial. However, this spokesperson did say that these initiatives came directly down from the former Attorney General Jeff Sessions under the strict instructions from President Donald Trump. The president was quoted as saying, "There is a serious issue with the disenfranchisement of White America and in order to make America great again, which is been my pledge ever since I was elected president, it starts by making all things equal. And unfortunately there are a lot of things that are not equal in America anymore, but we can fix that."

One of the biggest issues that have plagued America over the last decade is the rising numbers of white police officers shooting unarmed black citizens. The numbers have been at staggering high and in a lot of cases higher than they were during the Civil Rights Movement. But one thing the senior spokesman for the US Justice Department pointed out was that it's not like there wasn't a lot of violence going on at the time anyway. There just wasn't as many shootings of unarmed black citizens compared to lynchings.

However, after serious investigation, the Justice Department has come up with a solution as part of the president's new initiative on making all things equal. The Justice Department is now encouraging Black and Hispanic police officers to shoot unarmed White citizens during routine traffic stops. "It shouldn't be just unarmed black citizens getting shot, there should be an equal number of white citizens too, and it's only right if Black and Hispanic police officers do the shooting." This is a direct quote from the senior official at the US Justice Department.

Another major issue has been the disproportionate number of black men and women in prison for non-violent crimes such as drugs. This is mostly due to the mandatory minimum laws from the 1980s. Further reform has been a hot topic for more than two decades and even former President Bill Clinton has admitted that these mandatory minimum laws were wrong. But instead of getting rid of them, the US Justice Department has issued new guidelines when it comes to arresting suspects for non-violent crimes.   Police officers should arrest more white citizens for these crimes and prosecutors across the country should ask for jail time instead of probation. A senior Justice Department Official told me that if affirmative action can work for admissions to colleges and employment, then why it can't work for prisons. We should have an equal ratio of white and black men and women in prison for non-violent crimes with lengthy prison sentences.

For the last four election cycles, Voter ID laws have been another hot topic. In most States, especially in the Deep South, Voter ID laws were created to make sure, as lawmakers put it, that illegal immigrants and felons couldn't commit voter fraud. But the biggest complaint when it comes to Voter ID law is not the law itself, but it is the disproportionate ratio of elderly black men and women and some elderly white men and women who vote Democrat in the Deep South and may not have a photo ID because they were born before a time when birth certificates were easily created. For many years, Republican lawmakers have scoffed at the idea that Voter ID laws are unconstitutional and they disqualify many legal voters. Another new initiative by the US Justice

Department is not to get rid of these Voter ID laws, but to require that there are an equal number of Republican and Democrats being purged from voter lists for not having proper identification. While there have been always more Democrats that fall victim to Voter ID laws in the Deep South, the US Justice Department would require more Republican voters being a victim of Voter ID laws in heavily Democratic states such as New York and California. The Attorney General was quoted as saying, "Voter ID laws will always remain controversial; we shouldn't just get rid of these laws since they do serve a purpose. It's more important to have an equal number of American citizens who are affected by these laws. White, Black, and Hispanic citizens should equally be affected by these laws.

The last major issue the US Justice Department is tackling when it comes to the disenfranchisement of White America is how it deals with illegal immigration. Immigration is always a controversial subject in America and it seems like solutions are far and few as quoted by this senior Justice Department Official. He also said, "There may not be any long-term solutions to immigration and the wall may never get built because of the same old bureaucracy that plagues Washington DC, one of the things that we can do is not make illegal immigration so disproportionate among one ethnicity as in the case of Hispanics." There needs to be more white illegal immigrants in the United States. They need to come across the border in a different region of the United States such as Canada. The senior official also went on to say, "We may not be able to solve all the issues of immigration, but we can make it more equal among ethnicity and gender. The US Justice Department started a new initiative to get more illegal immigrants from Canada in order to equal the same amount of illegal immigrants coming from Hispanic countries." When I asked the senior official why this needed to happen, he quoted. "It may be a quick fix solution to immigration, but at least we will be equal in numbers which is more important when it comes to making America great again and stopping the disenfranchisement of White America. Plus, it would nice to use tear gas on illegal immigrants on both borders."

We all know there are many issues that plague American society, especially White America. The senior official for the US Justice Department told me that everything is being looked at, but this year we are tackling the four most important issues to help with this disenfranchisement of White America. If we can solve these issues, we should have no problem solving the other issues such as the equal number of employees working low paying jobs like Landscaping, picking fruits and vegetables in the fields of California and Florida, and fast food jobs. Why should these kind of jobs only be for minorities when there can be an equal number of Black, Hispanic, Asian, and white workers. I found this to be an interesting narrative by the US Justice Department to say the least. Perhaps our president is right…the first step in making America great again is making all things equal when it comes to criminals, the type of unarmed citizens who are being killed by police officers, and making sure that both Democrats and Republicans are equally affected by voter ID laws. Only time will tell if these new initiatives by the United States Justice Department will improve American society and stop the disenfranchisement of White America. But more importantly, will they make America great again!

Bob Jensen
Reporter & Columnist

The Squeeze
The more true news network!

Liberty
Since 2017!

500 FREE
Business Cards

*Premium Cards, 14pt Card Stock,
Full Color, Front and Back,
Glossy or Matte Finish*

Call Today
(888)
901-4665

www.bizproshop.com

Email us to find out how you can get 500 FREE business Cards. info@bizproshop.com or call (888) 901-4665

We are always looking for submissions. We are looking for Short Stories, Poetry, Editorials and Articles (Non Fiction) and Cartoons / Comic Strips.

Submit your work to www.starvingwriters.net

Email us your submissions at…

submission@starvingwriters.net